Why Parents Should Fear MySpace!

The Saga of Rick Rokr

First Edition

—⚯—

W.D.Edmiston, MSCJ

Why Parents Should Fear MySpace
by W.D.Edmiston, MSCJ

Printed in the United States of America

ISBN-13: 978-1-60034-992-8
IBSN-10: 1-60034-992-7

Scripture quotation was taken from the Old King James Version, printed in 1948 by Spencer Press, Chicago Illinois.

www.xulonpress.com

To those who helped make me an adult:
Julian Arlington South
J. Venson Roberts
IdaLee Derrett Edmiston

Special thanks to Ted and Mary Green
The best parents I know!

Why parents should fear MySpace!
By Woody Edmiston

CONTENTS

—ɯ—

Why parents should fear MySpace
The Saga of Rick Rokr

INTRODUCTION

—〰—

This book was researched and written on my son's computer. It is a place where he lived out the last weeks of his life. While sitting in this same chair he created an imaginary world that lead to his death. A social networking site allowed him to construct a completely fictional world; yet it was real to him. That life contained all of the things any young man would want. A short time later his world began to come apart. As a result he experienced all of the emotions and gut wrenching reactions as if it had happened in real life. He then took a course of action that we never expected: suicide.

The book is for parents. It is written as a warning that being on a social networking site is possibly dangerous for your child. Although it may seem improbable, the rest of this book is written to show you why it is true. I don't mean to tell you that a social networking site is going to cause your child to commit suicide. But sites such as these can influence kids and especially adolescent children who are just forming their identities. The events of his or her life may intertwine with ideas learned on a social networking site that result is sorrow, pain or suffering. I will attempt to show you how that can happen.

The purpose of my writing *is not* to place blame on MySpace, Tagworld, Facebook or any other online community for my son's death. I'm not trying to create a movement against anything. The purpose *is not* just to warn you about dangers presented by sexual predators who may try to meet your child. **The purpose *is* to make parents aware of a new cultural phenomenon and how it can affect adolescence.** Before my son's death, I thought that he was just spending a lot of time sending instant messages back and forth between friends. From my point of view it was no different from talking on the telephone. When I was a teen we would drag the phone into the closet so that we could talk to our friends for hours. I even argued with my wife that it was good for him to be making friends and spending time discussing life with them. There is a big difference between the two that I learned only after his death. As far as blame is concerned, I believe that the social networking sites come very close to being what in legal terms is called an **"attractive nuisance."** That is, something that has the potential of exposing a large number of people to danger — even if that was not the original purpose. I do believe that MySpace had a part in my son's death. I don't want it to have a part in any heartache for another family. Even so, this is not a diatribe against MySpace. *Peterbuilt makes a nice big truck. MySpace makes a nice advertising/communications device. Neither is particularly dangerous unless you don't know it's there and are hit by it*

The difficulty for me, as Ricky's parent, was that I did not know how much things had changed from the days when I stuttered and haltingly asked a little girl if she would be my steady. Had I known more about the sites I would have understood that the emotions he was experiencing were much deeper and much more sinister. He was not "just going through a phase" he was having a real emotional crisis.

In order for other parents to learn about social networking I will try to explain what social networking is and why it is different. I will tell you what I have learned in some 30 years of law enforcement, dealing with children's groups, scouting and working with children in foster care. I will also show you how these individual things work together to become a threat to children. At the end I will tell you the story of Ricky and how he became Rick Rokr. That tale should help you see how each element of the theory I propose came together to end his life. Someone may be able to make this point better or in a more straightforward way. They should write their own book.

These elements worked ***together*** to bring him to the point of crisis. I suspect he is not the only one. From what I have seen on social networking sites, other children are having trouble. My conclusions are that social networking is poorly understood and yet has the potential for culture wide impact — negative impact. My experiences also play their part in bringing me to those conclusions. Additionally, I have done research on the internet and elsewhere to find evidence to bolster my concerns. It is a complicated thesis. I hope you can take the time to understand and apply what you learn. In my opinion, allowing your children to use these spaces unmonitored is the equivalent of allowing them to walk down Bourbon Street at midnight in their pajamas.

Finally, I have spent most of my life dealing with some of the most disgusting topics and people imaginable as a part of being a police officer and investigator. I've been somewhat desensitized by it all. I'm well aware that some people may find reading about vulgar and suggestive topics unsettling. I have reduced the impact as much as possible by removing letters and trying to clean up examples of what you may see on SNS sites. I have no intention of offending anyone. This is a difficult area to investigate and read about. I apologize if you are unprepared or if you feel I should have left some things out. Nothing is included for shock value. I encourage every parent to spend some time investigating social networking sites. The sites are like life; multi-faceted, containing both the best and the worst of human traits.

Chapter One

DECEPTION AND TRUST

—⁂—

The September 2006 issue of Reader's Digest had a wonderful piece of art on the back cover. The scene is of a girl of the "tweener" age, sitting on her bed, surrounded by homework, an open laptop computer and the remains of snacks. She is talking on the telephone with her rosy cheeks reflecting the light of the computer screen. This is the image most people have of social networking or, as the artwork was titled: *My Space*.

Recently there has been a lot of discussion about the problem of children being harmed by people they meet online. Predators posing as teens have gotten sexual stimulation or lured children into illicit liaisons. What I want to point out is different. Your child can sit safely in the bedroom and construct an imaginary world full of friends they have never met. They can become involved in social networking to the point that they enjoy that life more than the one they share with you. Additionally, through social networking, they have the opportunity to learn about other ways of life and other values that are completely opposite of what you have been trying to teach them. All of this can take place under your nose if you let it. They are not yet equipped to handle this sort of exposure to life.

<u>This is important!</u>
Let this sink in: I am not talking about someone on the internet or SNS doing something to your child. Your children are adolescents. Their minds are open to all sorts of influences. The negative

ones begin with simple taunts and assaults on their personalities and extend to life style and thought processes that can have long term harmful effects. This is the main difference between what you will read elsewhere about the dangers of social networking. Most are talking about physical danger. [1] In this book I discuss dangers related to the formation of identity, personality, and lifestyles. The danger that concerns me is the manipulation of the **natural weaknesses of adolescence** by companies whose primary motive is to sell advertising. How did these companies craft a marketing plan so cleverly as to take advantage of those weaknesses? I don't know if it was by design or happenstance, but the effect is the same regardless the intent. Sites like these allow kids to create **online identities** at a time when they have not yet completely developed their personal identity and when they are highly impressionable and vulnerable. Adolescence is manipulated by the people, advertising and general culture of social networking. The effect can fundamentally change who your children will become as a result of changing how they form their identities. Everything you have taught your children will come into question as they meet people with different backgrounds. Your adolescent children are not ready to make a critical assessment of what they see and they have the curiosity to prowl throughout the social networking sites learning more about alternate lifestyles, deviate behavior, socio-political movements and socially unacceptable behavior. It's not their bodies I am worried about — it's their minds.

Loss of innocence

In an article in the Denver Post, a mother complained that the responses to her daughter's MySpace site drew criticism that shattered her innocence. The child suffered terrible pain as a result of a word battle with her peers. The mom happened to be a Psychotherapist with a Ph.D. and a newspaper columnist. In an article she wrote for the Post she talked about the ability of children to be cruel. She was amazed that a site existed that would allow so much acrimony. Her assessment of the site was:

"My daughter and her friends had gotten into an online war that left [her] and her parents hurt and embarrassed. [To resolve the issue] I had phone conversations with parents whom I had never met, as my daughter cried at the kitchen table. Someone had said something about someone, who had said something at the lockers about someone else, making up terrible lies about [each other] . . . How could this current upset have happened in the world of a child whose most risky behavior had been eating fast food two times a week and staying up past midnight? She was now passing devastating rumors instead of cards in Go Fish. Where did my daughter and her friends learn to verbally assault one another?"[2]

My answer to that question is: "Probably on a social networking site!" Online messaging appears to be the latest fad in a long line of fads. While this incident is one that the child will most likely get over, she will most likely not forget it.

Kids no longer want to fold little scraps of paper in class and hand them across several rows of their friends. They want to send the text message equivalent to a friend in the next class. They also want their own social networking space — sometimes called "a myspace."

What is it?

MySpace is multimillion dollar success. It is so successful and well known that, like Coca-Cola or Coke, their name: MySpace has become interchangeable for an entire product line. Having written and executed some marketing programs I am acquainted with how difficult that is to accomplish. I can't help admiring their success. Instant messaging and online chat have become such a sought after tool for social acceptance that many children will not stop talking about getting online until the parents relent. Ideally, he or she wants a laptop so they can sit in bed in their pajama's and chat. They also want a cell phone that allows text messaging. Text messaging is similar to the digital text pager. It allows short text messages to be sent from a computer or from another cell phone. The user can return "canned" messages prepared in advance, like: "Got ur msg.

Will call from next stop." The true text capable phones can send any message between them. They allow the users to respond without actually having a phone conversation. Since the phones can be made silent, a conversation can be had between users during a class or in the middle of a performance. If the phone also has a camera feature, the user can send a picture from a party they are attending with the text message: "We are having fun, why don't you come over?"

Too often for teens, the goal becomes obtaining as much electronic equipment as possible, Keep-Up-With-the-Joneses fashion, so they can constantly be in touch. You know, *just in case* a member of your group wishes to contact you. There is a further burden to actually have people call. If they don't then, you must not be all that popular.

The socialsoftwareweblog (www.socialsoftware.weblogsinc. com) bills itself as the Home of the Social Networking Services Meta List. It lists 380 different types of SNS with many different interest drivers. Those drivers may be pets, social meetings, dating or face-to-face facilitation (whatever that is?) The larger and more popular are, in no particular order: Facebook, Xanga, and MySpace. The last one, I'm told, is a part of the Rupert Murdoch conglomerate.

Defining Terms

Let me digress for a moment and discuss terms. MySpace refers to the company that offers this service to over 130 million subscribers. Social Networking Spaces (SNS) refers to all of the other sites that offer the service for sub-groupings of people or *users* to get to know each other and discuss topics of mutual interest. When the term myspace or myspaces is used, it also refers to a social networking site; but not always to MySpace. It's a bit confusing at first but watch the capital letters and you will catch on.

In order to understand what drives kids to want to be a part of social networking, you have to accept that there is something called "the scene." **The Scene** is a term originally used to refer to several networks of online groups that get new music, movies and games (at or before their public release) then illegally distribute them throughout the Internet. It has expanded to also include going to clubs to listen to the bands who play this music. Also part of The Scene is being able to *get in* to dance and party in exclusive nightclubs. It is sort of a status thing. One gets in based on style, having that certain something, or because of how one dresses, tends to his or her hairstyle and perhaps uses the right body spray. Scenesters, craft their lives around the ideas they get from movies and spend a great deal of time talking incessantly about concerts, music, movies, video games and dressing up for nights on the town. This too is a part of identity formation. It would seem that many children make being a part of The Scene their only goal in life even though they are not yet old enough to go into a nightclub. You may have seen commercials for clothing and soft drinks about young people waiting in line to get into trendy night clubs. Of course in the commercial the ones picked to get in are wearing the advertiser's clothes or drinking the advertiser's soda. This is an example of being a part of The Scene. In the case of the adolescent, they can't go to the clubs, but they want to appear to be part of the scene when they arrive at their school every morning. The only difference I found from my son wanting to be a part of all this hoo-ha was that he was willing to get out of bed 30 minutes earlier to carefully style his hair. It didn't make him any easier to get out the door on time.

How does it work?

The *space* or web page can be constantly changed. The user (your child) can add a different background or other decoration to his or her myspace. He or she can also add pictures and short video clips. The users post their favorite scenes from movies or television shows as well. There is a sub-grouping of marketers that sell clips and decorations to customize each site. Many users select music to play when you visit their site. The user will even list other songs and groups that are favorites. There is a window that allows the user to post personal bulletins. He or she can publish to their circle of friends an opinion article (called a Bulletin) about how stupid the school is to have a dress code or tell a tale of teenaged angst over having lost a love. They also tend to post some of the old stories we have all heard that amount to tired old urban legends. (There are new versions of The Hook and several of Teen Angel) Of course this is all done with the admonition that it is the absolute truth as told by a friend. The user also posts a series of likes and dislikes reminiscent of the old Dewar's Profiles or the stats of a sports celebrity. *For girls it is an interactive doll house and all her friends can play. For boys it is a scrapbook that just happens to have its own background music.* It is a creation that defines them; their online identity. The kids post the site for old and new friends and let them take a look at their creation. Each friend then posts a comment. The people who offer the service want you to think the conversations are something like: "You look really nice in that outfit!" or "Don't you think Tiffany and Bobby make a cute couple?" "Are you going to the game? *If they were just talking about this sort of thing I wouldn't be writing this book.*

Free for nothing

You can become a part of this phenomenon for free. Subscriptions cost nothing. They allow the subscribers to post their favorite art, pictures, and a short biography. You post your picture on the site with a short bit of wisdom that encapsulates who you are. At another place in your space you post a list of likes and dislikes. The format is Q&A e.g. Have you ever kissed someone? | Yes, my boyfriend! The goal for each user is to put his or her "best foot forward" so to speak. The audience of other users is supposed to look at each offering and make complimentary or constructive comments. The primary goal is to be complimented on *how you look.* Therefore there are always pictures of the user on the site. Photos are usually taken with the user's camera phone. If the other user likes your look or finds something you have in common he or she can request that you be "friends." The whole thing is sort of a 21st century version of video dating that was so popular a few years ago. But unlike dating services, there is no assumption that the two will actually meet. They are supposed to be friends in cyberspace. The only ones that you meet in person are already friends. It does allow those friends to introduce others.

These websites are lately being aimed at a much younger group. My best intelligence info tells me that sites will soon be marketed to a pre-adolescent market. The latter two groups (pre-adolescents and adolescents) are not, most parents would say, quite ready to date. The large majority of the subscribers are girls aged 12 to 17 if you are to judge from what I see on Ricky's site. As a general rule the boys on the sites tend to be more computer geek than sports jock. The whole focus of the sites is pretty much geared to dating and talking about who is "hott."

One might think that if the kids never actually meet there is very little danger involved. I would have to agree with relation to physical harm. But look further at the SNS' and what there is to experience in a vicarious fashion and you will see more danger. Of course I mean dangerous, in the sense of overexposure to more adult matters.

Being part of "The Scene"

Young kids often try to grown up too fast. They also tend to look up to older siblings or those only slightly older; certainly not *old* adults. For that reason they do things without the application of common sense. There is nothing particularly new about younger children getting in trouble trying things that are not age appropriate: cigarettes behind the wood shed, taking the car for a spin when your parents are not home. What happens on myspaces is a bit different, but not a lot. The temptation to be a part of this scene is becoming so important to some children that they are taking risks and engaging in behavior well beyond their ability to manage. Their conversations, bulletins and questionnaires are usually pretty spicy. A high number of the users post pictures that are suggestive. Oftentimes kids, who are not yet able to drive, are partially if not totally nude in some of their "pics." Pics, short for the pictures folder, is a part of the SNS where the user can post the latest pictures they have taken. They change or add to them regularly. They pose in ways that cover the more illicit areas but tease nonetheless. Boys and girls kiss and snuggle; sometimes in swimwear. Girls often kiss each other or pose in a sexually suggestive manner. One of the most popular poses is from overhead looking directly down upon the girl. The girls make a point of wearing low cut outfits in pics that reveal a lot of cleavage. Once these pictures are posted on the SNS they are out there for others to see almost indefinitely. The reason for all of this titillation is to spice up their site and garner an ever increasing circle of "friends on myspace." To be deleted as a friend or demoted from the inner circle of friends can be cause for histrionics.

SNS and Anorexia

There is a lot of talk on SNS that relates to body image. The pictures of the girls that I see posted on these sites are a slice of Americana. Many are little girls who are still growing. Some of them are obviously emotionally and physically immature. When you read their sites you find that way too many of them are looking at themselves and drawing irrational conclusions about being too fat or having faulty features. Anorexia, an eating disorder, results when girls become obsessed with their body image. The causes for anorexia are very complex, but one factor is sociological. By that I mean that many professionals see the promotion of the super thin female as the ideal body type as a social factor of Anorexic behavior. The desire to be thin, as she assumes the idealized image of woman-hood to be, drives a girl to seek that body type. This idealized image is often supported by peer relationships, television and reading teen magazines. One finds no comfort on a SNS from the participants or even close friends. Because the spaces are private communication any discussion of weight and eating becomes personal. Anorexia has one of the higher mortality rates of any psychiatric disorder.

Pooling their ignorance

Equally dangerous is that the kids tend to speak of their values and philosophies of life on SNS. These philosophies can be a mish-mash of knowledge floating about in the ether of the teen cosmos or things they learn from adults. This is a process that I have termed: pooling their ignorance. Once their minds are made up about a topic, they speak in hyperbole and in very concrete terms. They are "forever" in love, their boyfriend/girlfriend is the "best" ever, they are "unique" and no one in the world ever thought and acted like they do. They want the best and refuse to compromise. They begin sentences with defining phrases: "If you want to know about me. . . ." and "This is what I am like . . ." These are all attempts to quantify and validate their identity. They seem to think that a personality can be defined with a few simple terms. They use multiple choice questionnaires about likes and dislikes that simultaneously create somewhat inconsistent codes of conduct. When they pass these questionnaires between themselves they are also sending the message that the choices are the most logical or accepted responses. By assigning that weight to those responses they are defining right and wrong. Not all these philosophies come from children — they come from adults with ulterior motives. They can be inconsistent because adolescents still retain the ability (or disability) to think magically. The tendency to perpetuate and give them weight in hyperbole is a characteristic of adolescence.

Pay attention to the questionnaires

Go back and read the last paragraph and pay attention to what I said about the questionnaires. It's easy to skip over the question-naires and not appreciate how important they are in this process. They have the effect of creating a code of conduct. That means the rules we live by. When you read an example of a questionnaire later in this book you will see that they can redefine right and wrong by modeling behavior. One kid circulating these at a school in Peoria is not going to make a lot of difference. But one kid placing them on an SNS that is seen by thousands of kids and then reposted to even more — probably will.

As a member of a society, group or community, your child can hold both a personal value system and a communal value system at the same time. In this case, the two value systems (one personal and one communal) are **externally consistent** provided they bear no contradictions or situational exceptions between them. That is the kind of system that parents strive for when they choose neighbor-hoods and schools that they think will reflect their values. A value system in its own right is **internally consistent** when its values *do not contradict* each other and its exceptions are: *abstract* enough to be used in all situations; and *consistently* applied. SNS' do not necessarily have internally consistent values because they change depending upon who your child is chatting with. Therefore you have no way of predicting how your child will interpret what they hear.

This is important!

If your child has both a home computer and a phone capable of instant messaging, he or she is outfitted for the current generation. This generation is not just in touch with the kids at school. They are in touch with kids from around the world. The social networking sites are easily accessed with any late model computer, as are the instant message sites. For this generation mobility is the key. The chief aim of a myspace scenester is to be constantly entertained and always plugged in to the latest happenings. They want to be constantly doing things, but want to be constantly in touch with the circle of friends they feel are most important. Since the introduction of the messaging centers like MySpace, Xanga, Facebook, and Tagworld social network users have the opportunity to approach relationships in a new way. This can be done using electronic devices. Those of you who remember the citizen band radio craze that occurred when C.B. McCall sang about his convoy and Burt Reynolds was filming *Smokey and the Bandit* (1983) are familiar with how that sort of thing can happen. We "knew" Digger Dan or Pistol Pete and liked to talk to them on our CB radios when they came through town. We never actually met them, but somehow we shared a small slice of our lives with them. Conversing on SNS is very similar.

Always in touch

There are email sites specifically for myspace users. The cyber spaces link user's email and text messaging to the SNS on the home computer. While he or she is away from the computer, a person on a computer at some other location can send a message that connects to the computer and then the user's cell phone. The text message tells him or her that they got an email or message on the networking space. With the right (read as expensive) phone they can both read and *respond* to the email. Therefore if he really embraces this medium your child is never truly away from their space. Even when they are riding in the car with you or sitting in the classroom, they are accessible. This is why many schools have already stopped allowing kids to bring cell phones to school and have outlawed using social networking websites on school computers.

You have a friend request

Try to envision how this happens at your house. Picture your child sitting in front of the computer having previously set up a social networking page and an instant message account linked to email. If your child is on an email site, surfing the internet or, out of necessity doing homework, messages continually pop up in the lower corner of their screen. It tells them they have someone asking to be their "friend" or a friend is available to talk on the social networking site. While they are on the internet looking up information for that term paper you have been encouraging them to complete — messaging continues. Little windows relentlessly pop up in the lower right hand side of the screen announcing that a "buddy" is signing on or off the computer. There is always a temptation to reply. Your child is constantly being summoned by people who have no idea that he or she is supposed to be writing a history paper. And they don't care. They are asking to be entertained. Your child's concentration will be splattered and don't be surprised if his or her grades drop. At some point you are going to be using the word "obsession" a lot. Using the sites is new, it's exciting and the kids get "hooked" quickly.

Let me stop right here and make a statement. My personal belief is that if you allow your son or daughter, an internet capable computer in their **bedroom** *you are out of your mind!* If you allow them to do internet surfing, Instant Message (IM) and social networking some place where you cannot watch them you are losing the battle for your kids. Computers belong in some common area of the home. You must make it a point to be aware of who they are talking to and what they are learning from their conversations.

Why is this so attractive?

A social networking site is a place free from adult interference for the most part. Children like my son, are free to be as goofy or real in cyberspace as they choose. They expect to be entertained by their friends and to participate in entertainment. It is the young person's equivalent of the groups of kids that used to hang out at malt shops. Instead of kids in Levi's sitting around on the back of their cars and trucks, it is a hundred million young people sitting in their pajamas at a hundred million computers tied together into one common "space." The parents only know that they are quiet and safe in their own bedrooms. Most of them would think that it is better than sitting around with a bunch of kids on a parking lot. But is this really true? I'll talk more about that later in the book.

What is on a myspace, space?

Entering the site, the home page offers you the opportunity to meet new people. They are even tagged with a notice if they are "on-line now." When I look at the "new" people that are "online now" I can go to their site, read their biography and take a look at their pictures. To be honest, the majority of them are just kids of varying ages who want to entertain themselves by poking around in the lives of other people. You look at the other kid's pictures and read their profiles to find out what you have in common. If they are the kind who likes to write, you may get a chance to read a few paragraphs about their visit to a concert. Most of them are kids in school clothes who have created sites to honor friends they "really, really luv" or post pictures they took at the last football game. Most of the girls come across as just a little "boy crazy." The boys on SNS are for the most part pretty thoughtful. There are a lot of band members and boys who play instruments. Since one of the main functions of MySpace is to promote bands, it stands to reason that there would be a lot of musicians. Other sites promote other things.

How long do you think it takes to find someone nude or nearly nude? Well, if you count the girls that are on the edges of the screen advertising dating clubs, no longer than it takes to log on. After that you are free to check out other personal sites and ask others to be your friend. Once you get rolling, you may find that by looking through these pages there are some very slick, professional photographs that aren't quite like the others. When the photo looks professional it is often thinly disguised connection to pornography presented as a myspace site. Every once in a while a page will come up on one of these that warns, "Don't enter unless you are 18 years of age." Of course there seems to be no universal responsibility on the part of the person creating that site to either post the message or enforce the rule. All your 15 year old has to do is check a box that "certifies" that he is over 18.

When you enter the individual sites you find a mish-mash of ideas. They pool their limited knowledge of life and regurgitate ideas that sound like a beer commercial, Ben Franklin's *Poor Richard* or some rock star's view of life. Often, that has something to do with sex! Below is a listing of a few random scenesters that I found with a few minutes clicking.

Note: the difference between a personal space and a public space is that the former can be set to be viewed only by specific friends the user selects. A public space might also be created for people who have tattoos or a band to promote their music. The examples below are composites.

Damaged Dolz: Who is a broken doll? (public space)

"A DD is the girl who is secure in herself and does as what she wants. She is unconcerned about the rules and regulations of the world around her. She has strength, charisma and personality. Each "Doll" is beautiful in her own way and loves to flaunt that beauty to the world. She is creating art with her presence in daily life. The prudes would deem this as not a woman's place, therefore making her "broken" by society's standards. But, she doesn't care about what society thinks. She offers herself here for the entire World to taste her creation."

What follows is a gallery of nearly nude, tattooed girls who could be anywhere from 15 to 25. As far as I know, there is no way of determining if the rules that apply to pornography (regarding age of those photographed) apply to these personal sites.

Asian Fantasyland – under the heading of cultural sites. (public space)

"A place for anyone who loves Asian culture. It's about food, actors, models, TV, movies, anime, martial arts, etc!! Anything. Use this group to meet and talk to anyone who also has similar interests."

Clicking on the site and scrolling down to the photographs took only a couple of seconds to find near-nude models in suggestive photos. One of these included two females embracing in a sexual way.

Sleazy and Proud. (A personal space)

The personal web space of someone who says she is 19 years old, living in New York. Her idea of fun is having sex constantly and she will talk about that on line with whoever asks. The photographs were all of different parts of her nude body. I'll not go into details. You get the drift, the name says it all.

K_____ (personal space)

"For you, kissing is all about following your urges. If someone's hot, you'll go in for the kiss - end of story. You can keep any relationship hot with your steamy kisses. A total spark plug - your kisses are bound to get you in trouble."

K_____ is 18 and her bio, Q&A says that she has showered with someone of the opposite sex, slept with someone of the opposite sex, has stayed online more than five hours, and likes athletic or muscular men. When asked her preference between opposites she offered the following:

bud or coors? **Bud**
cope or skoal? **Cope**
do it for the buckle or the girls/guys? **Buckle**
beef or pork? **Beef**
hunting or fishing? **Hunting**
drugs or jesus? **Jesus**
stetson or resistol? **Stetson**
bed of your truck or a motel? **Truck**

What concerns me with these responses is that she seems to have some knowledge of Jesus (one would presume Christianity as well) and prefers him over drugs – but doesn't let that get in the way of a pretty promiscuous life! This is a contradictory message. I would rather that my son or daughter not get the idea that one can be Godly and sexually active at the same time. Contradictory messages have run amok on SNS.

An electronic tree house

The social networking site allows your teenager to have a private conversation while sitting smack in the middle of that space where you think you are in control. Actually you are supposed to be in control but social networking changes the level of control you can enforce. Instant messaging allows a more private conversation than we got when we dragged the phone into the closet. Being in touch inside a social networking site allows the user to be in touch with thousands of people while being completely private from prying eyes or parental oversight. It's sort of an electronic tree-house — No Parents Allowed. This characteristic is the reason your child should not be using the computer in the bedroom. It is also the reason that you have to know what to expect from social networking or you won't realize the source of the changes in attitude you see in your children.

Is this space a place?

One of the more interesting discussions that I have read about virtual spaces is whether or not they are "space" at all. These sites are said to be "digital publics" and understanding them and finding your way through them is new for most people. (Federman, 2006) Is something that exists in the electronic memory of a computer network spatial in nature? You can answer that question when you realize the space is "imagined space." I would offer that the similarity is much like the "place" we go to when we are gazing out the window on a hot spring day in the back row of English class. Didn't your children's grandparents warn you about that — getting lost in your imagination? We were told that spending all our time daydreaming would make us unproductive adults. Although we celebrate the fanciful imaginations of Stephen King or Dr. Seuss, few parents want their children permanently lost in a state of daydreaming.

If one takes a look at the creator of MySpace's personal site you find that he is relatively young. Tom occasionally, sends bulletins to everyone on MySpace about things he finds interesting. Recently he broadcast a video of a girl dancing at a party while holding on to a pole at the edge of a stage. She becomes so involved in her dancing that she accidentally tumbles off of the stage. The caption to the video said something to the effect of: "This girl thinks she is so cool. Ha Ha. She fell of the stage, she's not that cool!" Personally, I don't need adults, acting like kids, perpetuating ideas about class envy or assigning motivation to the acts of others without good evidence. This sort of thing is exactly what we try to teach our children not to do. The effect of having a warehouse for bad manners, dumb ideas and an adult to distribute them is deleterious to those teens who participate. If these warehouses promoted positive role modeling it would be different. But they don't!

In my personal opinion, all the social networking site promoters are somewhat aware that the sites could be dangerous to young people. However, if they have no training in social work, child psychology or have never lived with an adolescent; there is no reason for them to know. Even if they give it a thought, most of them just think it is, at worst, a sort of really scary fun sort of like going to the Rocky Horror Picture Show. They seem willing to continue selling advertising and promoting the use of these sites.

Real serious social networking site users, especially those who follow MySpace, will say that I am forgetting the important part the internet and social networking plays in getting unknown bands an opportunity to be discovered. I haven't. First, it's not all that important to the points I am making about the manipulation of adolescence. Second, most of what I have said about the negative aspects of the social networking sites and the belief systems they promote applies to the music, the names the bands give themselves and the lifestyles they promote.

Accountability

A myspace user can say anything or make any claim without any accountability. Like everything on the internet, there is no central place that verifies the truth of any matter discussed. When we have face-to-face conversations with our friends, we tend to be accountable and expect that they are accountable based on the fact that we are going to bump into each other regularly. If my neighbor tells me something about himself, that he drives a sports car for instance, I have little trouble verifying that fact. We will seldom meet the people from the Internet and myspace. Even if we cross paths we won't recognize them. Therefore the temptation to inflate our identity a bit is persuasive. People who want to mislead are equally aware that there is no way to check facts. That means there is little you can trust. There is nothing that truly enforces responsibility or ensures that those who use the spaces are trustworthy.

A good cussin'

If someone dares to voice the opinion that myspaces should be better controlled; they are instantly challenged. The users will attack with venom. A tirade of vulgar language will be directed at anyone (on a blog or in email) who dares question the "goodness" or safety of using these spaces. The following was taken from an unidentified site and recreated, mistakes and all. It is illuminating!

" u guys spend way too much time in ur childerns lives…. stope with all [the we hate] google.com** s—t. . . .give ur children some space no wonder they hate u…do u still change there underwear for them? I wish I could have a loving over-reacting bunch like u on myspace so I could spam the s— outta you . . do u feel stupid yet?"

**Google owns MySpace and supplies GMail the site specific email.

This kid should have been paying more attention to his spelling and grammar homework. It is a stereotypically vulgar and illiterate response to a rather objective critique of social networking spaces by Daniel Morgan posted April 23rd, 2006. It was found in a search of social networking sites.

http:moneydick.com/wordpress/2006/04/23/science-of-myspace/

The point: **You can expect major difficulty with your child if you approach his or her use of social networking sites with the attitude that you will just stop them from using it.**

First of all, you are asking for a fight that, even if you win, you won't enjoy the victory.

Second, I'm not sure that it would be a good thing. Being fluent in the technology that the next generation will use to communicate is important. One must learn to use it properly and with good citizenship. In his recent book, T. J. Waters describes what happened following the attacks in New York on September 11, 2001. A lot of patriotic, electronic communications minded young business people went to work for the Central Intelligence Agency in response to the tragedy. Roughly 40% of the people, who work there now, are familiar with multi-function cell phones, computer communication and information sharing. The older group of people who had worked for the agency prior to that time were much more used to the memo and written communication. In an October 28, 2006 interview on the Fox Network, he said this has helped to change the characteristic of the agency as an insular, non-communicative agency to one that understands the latest technology and values information sharing. (Waters, 2006) The U.S Navy has a new generation of swift boats that are driven with a joy stick instead of a more traditional ships wheel. It has allowed new recruits to adapt to handling the boats during maneuvers faster and with better control. A plowboy from Kansas at the outset of WWII was more able to go from tractor wheel to ship's wheel. Today's gaming enthusiast is more adept at the joystick than the steering wheel. A child who grows up understanding information sharing technology is going to be better equipped to compete in the future job market.

The technology will remain and expand in the future but we must eventually civilize the way we treat each other and communicate socially. Right now, the character of cyberspace is uncontrolled, un-watched, used by everyone from teens to terrorists. The cyber world has the quality of a red light district in a gold rush town, the saloon scene in Star Wars, and the streets of Chicago in the roaring twenties, all rolled into one easy to use entryway. Right now our kids are neck deep in it.

Third, being involved with SNS has some elements related to how adolescents form loyalty to their friends. They are apt to be very protective of the ability to communicate with them. This is one of those places where it would be wise to pick your battle site. The fear you have for you child's safety should be moderated by allowing some supervised risk taking. That's why you are reading this book.

MySpace and criminal behavior

Any place that offers kids the opportunity to get together is an opportunity for them to engage in risky behavior. This leads me to mention something about this group that few people outside of Criminology or Criminal Justice know or care about. For purposes of understanding the vulnerability of kids of adolescent age, one should understand that this group has historically been connected to bad behavior. Most kids are carefully watched until they reach this age. During adolescence they begin to go places on their own, drive and socialize with less restriction. The minute they get out of the house, about 12 to 20% run headlong into law enforcement and the courts. One reason is that children this age are not yet fully socialized. The age group takes risks, does not think ahead and in easily preoccupied. In my case, as it is with many others, I was too young to exercise good judgment. Therefore, I had an auto accident the night I got my drivers license. On top of that I stretched the truth when I explained how it happened to my mother. I was grounded for thirty days. I'm just fortunate that I did not try the same story on the police officer.

You need to know that criminal activity has been studied for years. If one compares data relating age to criminal activity from the late 19th century with similar studies from this century you will find that they are essentially the same. That is, most crime is committed by children from mid-teens to mid-twenties. Historically, having been sampled time and again back as much as 300 years, this age group has been prone to dangerous and anti-social behavior. In the 20th century the base of the Bell Curve had a tendency to broaden, bringing in more young teens. A **standard normal distribution** is often called the **bell curve** because the graph of its probability density resembles a bell. In an age graph the base of the curve would be wider if the ages related to crime were 12 through 24 as opposed to being more narrow if they were 14 to 24. You can thank gangs for that change. Historically, and in the present day, more crimes are committed by this age group. The advent of social networking will, I predict, produce more opportunity for children in this bracket to offend and to commit crimes with a higher degree of preparation and conspiratorial conduct.

The internet, and websites such as <u>Myspace</u> and <u>Xanga</u>, which are designed specifically to build networks, like those between David Ludwig and Kara Beth Borden, may increase crime rate. They create a new "Small World Phenomenon," and spread information quickly – and sometimes fatally. Is it appropriate to ban students from myspace? A good question, especially in light of this new double murder... I think such an interference with privacy would be met with outrage, but perhaps it is important merely for rules to be firmly set in households like those of Ludwig and Borden. If Ludwig had been kept under more monitoring, and had received positive reinforcement for good behavior, I wonder if he would have loved pranks and getting in trouble.(sic) Maybe two parents would not be dead and a young girl would not have been influenced to accomplice a murder.

It is important to note that much very critical political and social information is spread through networking sites like these... and that they shape language and future thought processes indefinitely.

Glamourous on Fri, 2005-11-18 19:25.
Web of Influence a student project of Bryn Mawr College.

The above quote is related to an incident in which a much younger girl fell in love with a boy from an online connection. The specific SNS they used is unknown. As the story was reported on CNN, Ludwig 18 and Borden 14 met online and began to date. Her parents did not want her to date him because of the age difference. After a short courtship, her parents tried to end the relationship. In an adolescent frenzy they concocted a plan to murder her parents and run away. After a night of being out together, according to those reports, they returned early in the morning and murdered both her parents. Like most of these stories it ended when police found them in another state.

The speaker in the quote above asks valid questions: Would stronger household rules have helped? What if the David Ludwig had been better supervised? The speaker also gives a title to the phenomenon that I describe in this book. The small world phenomenon is the same as I have, and will continue to discuss, in this book. Social networking sites offer the opportunity for its users to create a separate life, an imaginary world that still carries all of the emotion of real life. When those emotions spill out into the real world, like they did in this case, the consequences are tragic.

Things may be larger than they appear

The FBI Compiles a Uniform Crime Report (UCR) annually from reports drawn from police agencies around the country. They also make a predictive analysis of crime to compensate for the natural under reporting of crime due to fear, being too busy or shame. The conclusions are logically drawn as a result of research and testing. The UCR statistics report produced every year by the FBI and local law enforcement is for *reported crimes.* The FBI also produces statistics based on unreported crimes using a method that extrapolates survey data based on known characteristics of those crimes and their victims. The National Criminal Victimization Survey gives them a better picture of the true crime rate. Sexual crimes are one of the least well reported crimes. In this case I am referring to things like rape and incest. Crimes involving willing participants in a sexual act between older and younger persons are even less well reported. In fact they are seldom discovered. One of the persistent sexual fantasies that men report is between themselves and their babysitters or teachers. One can assume that it is not always a fantasy. The actual number of crimes in some of these categories may be three to five times higher than they are reported. Since it is not illegal to cause harm by use of the internet yet, how well reported can instances of harm be? If they are not being reported or are poorly reported — how protective do we have to be as parents to keep our kids safe?

Defining Social Networking or myspace Sites as Public places

There are few scholarly things written about SNS. On one site I read a discussion that I found intriguing: Is an online site a public

33

place? Social networking spaces are definitely open to the public. In a public street there are things that you cannot do without offense. One of the more common photographs added to a kid's social networking site is one taken with a digital camera in the mirror of his or her bathroom. The reason for this is that most users are alone when they are plugged into the alternate reality of the social networking space. They don't have anyone at hand to help them take a picture and they certainly are not going to have their parents do it. Often they appear partially nude to spice up the interest in their site. If, for instance, you take off all or part of your clothing and begin to take pictures of yourself in the mirror of the department store, public officials will intercede. But, this same thing is done in bathroom mirrors and broadcast on social networking sites daily. What is also true is that any policing of these sites is going to run smack dab into the First Amendment guarantees of free speech. Before you can determine if a thing is a violation of the law you must first give the activity a good definition. That has not yet been done.

What would be a good definition of a social networking site? Let's look at what some users on the Urban Dictionary said about MySpace:

> "Very strong internet crack."
>
> "A place to write pointless, overly wordy, bad descriptions of your daily life as if anyone is interested ... a complete lack of self awareness is required to continue on as a myspace addict."
>
> "A site purely developed to make you feel like s__. A huge popularity contest."
>
> "A site where you can find anyone you want, simply by clicking on other people's myspaces until you find someone you think is hot. Then once you're their friend you feel like you know so much about them and you've never even met them before."
>
> http://www.urbandictionary.com

This is my definition of social networking: **"One of any number of commercial computer sites created by major and minor corporations, the primary purpose of which is to create a vehicle**

for advertising. This is done by offering a social intercourse site to appeal to as wide an audience as possible without regard to the benefits or dangers of participation."

I'm not counting on the industry adopting my definition any time soon! WDE

I hate my parents

Parents, church leaders, scoutmasters, den mothers, teachers and the like are all working to help children grow. In the past we had the help of a cohesive society that had been successfully parented. They grew up in agreement with, and knew how to reinforce, the education you are giving your child. There is enough dissension about what is right and wrong in society today that you no longer have that assurance. Thanks to the number of peoples who never matured, (see a later chapter for the definition of PVA) mass marketing and agenda driven groups that promote social change, **this society is more polarized than it has been in any time since the Civil War.**

The blogger, Moneydick, wrote an article researching MySpace in April of 2006. In that article he conducted searches on MySpace sites. At that time there were 72,000,000 subscribers. As I write today, there are over 130,000,000. In his research he found some interesting things. He first complained that these sites tend to eliminate any accepted standard for spelling. This is a factor that I have, until now, ignored in this book. However, there is a distinct language and pervasive use of acronyms that the users must memorize in order to communicate. I find it to be a lesser problem but somewhat disturbing. There is also the penchant for using what he calls "cookie cutter phrases" like lol or omfg that he finds particularly irritating and annoying. What I found most interesting is that he sorted for "I hate my mom/mother" or "I hate my dad/father" or "I hate my parents" and found that 16.7% of the spaces contained these phrases. Ouch! At that rate, your child has the opportunity to exchange notes with 21,700,000 other children who hate their parents; if this blogger is accurate. I have no doubt that he is pretty close. This can only serve to justify and reinforce their feelings. These feelings are common in adolescence and usually fade quickly. However, if your child has a good deal of reinforcement for those feelings from online peers the attitude can become more ingrained. What will be the result or what will be their response? I can only guess that it will be like a snow-flake — unique. As has already been established elsewhere in this dissertation, they are more likely to believe and emulate their peers.

The list below gives you a sampling of myspace SNS acronyms. A perusal of those and their meanings is instructive. My personal favorite is P911.

Social Networking Acronyms

AFAIK - As Far As I Know

AFK - Away From the Keyboard

AFN - that's All For Now

AOTA - All Of The Above

AV Avatar - A picture often used in chat rooms and bulliten boards to give a unique identity.

b4 - Before

BAK - Back At Keyboard (I'm back)

BBL - Be Back Later

BBS - Be Back Soon

BCNU - I'll Be Seeing You.

b/f - Boyfriend (also shown as bf, B/F, or BF)

BEG - Big Evil Grin

BFN - Bye For Now

BTW - By The Way

wbt - BeTWeen you and me ...

CU - See You - also known as cya

CUL8R - See You Later

CUOL - See You On Line

CYA - See Ya

DIKU - Do I Know You?

EOT - End Of Thread (meaning end of discussion)

ez or **EZ** - easy

F2F - Face To Face

FAQ - Frequently Asked Question

FITB - Fill In The Blanks

FOCL - Falling Off Chair - Laughing

FUBAR - "Fouled" Up Beyond All Repair / Recognition

FUD - Fear, Uncertainty, and Doubt

FWIW - For What It's Worth

FYI - For Your Information

GAL - Get A Life

g/f - Girlfriend (also shown as gf, G/F, or GF)

GFN - Gone For Now

GGOH - Gotta Get Outta Here

GTR - Got To Run

GTRM - Going To Read Mail

H&K - Hugs and Kisses

HAGD - Have A Good Day

HAGO - Have A Good One

HB - Hurry Back

HTH - Hope That Helps

IDN - I Don't kNow

IDK - I Don't Know

IDTS - I Don't Think So

IC - I See

IMHO - In My Humble Opinion (or In My Honest Opinion)

IMO - In My Opinion

IOH - I'm Out of Here

IOW - In Other Words

JK - Just Kidding

JMO - Just My Opinion

JW - Just Wondering
KIT - Keep In Touch
LMAO - Laughing My A** Off
LFFAO - Laughing My
    F***(freaking) A** Off
LOL - Laughing Out Loud
LYL - Love You Lots
nm, - or **NM** Never Mind
NP, np - No Problem
OBTW - Oh, By The Way.
OIC - Oh, I See
OMG - Oh My Gosh
OT - Off Topic
OTOH - On The Other Hand ...
P911 -My parents are in the room.
PITA -Pain In The A**
PLZ -Please
PMJI - Pardon Me for Jumping In
POS - Parents are looking Over my
    Shoulder.
POTS - Parents Over The Shoulder
QT - Cutie
ROFL - Rolling On Floor, Laughing
ROTF - Rolling On The Floor
    (laughing is implied)
ROTFLMAO - Rolling On The Floor
Laughing My A** Off
ROTFLMFAO - Rolling On The
    Floor Laughing

SOTA - State Of The Art (latest
    technology)
SPST - Same Place, Same Time
SSDD - Same S**t, Different Day
SYL - See You Later
TAFN - That's All For Now
TC - Take Care
TFH - Thread From Hell
TIA - Thanks In Advance
TMI - Too Much Info. (information)
TNT - 'Til Next Time
TPS - That's Pretty Stupid
TS - Tough S**t
TTFN - Ta-Ta For Now
TTYL - Talk To You Later
TY - Thank You
TYT - Take Your Time
TYVM - Thank You Very Much
US - You Suck
WEG - Wicked Evil Grin
WEU - What's Eating You?
WFM - Works For Me
WIIFM - What's In It For Me?
WTG - Way To Go
WTGP? - Want To Go Private?
    (go to a private chat room)
WWJD - What Would Jesus Do?
YBS - You'll Be Sorry
YL - Young Lady

Trust

If there is a place where trust is poorly placed it is cyberspace. The users, as I previously mentioned, create a sort of scrapbook for themselves on the space. However, what is in each of those scrapbooks is a creation of either:

1. the truth;
2. the users version of the truth,
3. the wishful thinking of the user and what he would like to be the truth, or;
4. A fanciful and harmless exaggeration of the truth.

In the more egregious category are depictions that are:

5. Outright lies being put forth as the absolute truth.

In that latter category are those people who are the worst of the worst in cyberspace, those who would prey on less able and trusting people. I'm not just talking about pedophiles. We have all heard of pedophiles who are posing as 15 year old boys to lure young girls into meeting them. Pedophiles actually are only interested in children not yet having come into puberty. The term for these freakazoids is more correctly *Ephebophilia* in the case of adolescent girls and *pederasty* in the case of boys. In either case you don't want your kid involved.

One would think the girls surely know better than to meet someone that they hardly know alone. But such is not the case. In my last year as police chief in a small central Texas community, we investigated the report of two missing 12 year old girls. After they were found, we disentangled them from this story. On Friday afternoon on a holiday weekend, they hitched a ride to the local Wal-Mart. Their plan was to hang out in front of the store until they met some boys. Their plan was to "party" all weekend. They posted their plan on a website at school. They found two 19 year old boys who they had never met before. Together the foursome spent the weekend skinny dipping in the lake, having sex with multiple partners and drinking. When our officers found them, the girl's wet, lace, string bikini panties were still lying on the floorboard of the truck. (They were 12; their undies should have still had Dora the Explorer on them) The girls had hatched this plan because one of them was already pregnant by a 21 year old neighbor. She just wanted to have some fun before she started "showing" and had to tell her parents. The girls planned to raise the child together.

The ones who are lured to these liaisons are not just teenaged girls. I described earlier how easy it is to go from my own home page to that of some pretty unsavory characters. While on the home page, there are opportunities to sample the pages of new members. One that I chose at random offered me the opportunity to talk to a 34 year old guy in another state who had a video camera and liked voyeurism and bondage. The gay community has some opportunists and predators as well. There is ample opportunity for either hetero-sexual or homosexual banter, sharing of photographs and online mutual masturbation; and I mean that literally. If you go to a standard home page on a myspace and sort through the "new" users you will shortly find one that looks like a typical teen but is everything but typical. In the Appendix, I have placed an example of this sort of space. (See: "Hi, I'm Lola") It is not reading for the faint of heart but it is easily accessible by any teen. But, as I will describe to you later, this is not the only place that trust becomes an issue. The advertisers are violating a trust as well.

Culture Clash

In a recent Sunday School class, I listened as one of the leaders explained the changes in youth terminology that she encountered when she addressed a group of young women. The group was planning a trip to an area of another state to help in a mission program. She encouraged the girls to bring their swimsuits and thongs to wear around the pool. She explained that they would have the opportunity to swim at the hotel pool and that they would need thongs because the temperature would be over 100; the concrete would be hot. The leader, a wonderful lady in her forties, forgot that "thongs" and "cheap sandals" no longer mean the same thing when one of the girls told her, "My mother won't let me wear a two-piece much less a thong!"

Sex Ed: Street level

In my early years most of the talk about sex came from older peers. I first heard about it when I worked part time at gas station jobs and when I had my newspaper route. I remember a young fellow who always dressed like "The Fonz" from the old Television show, Happy Days. He seemed to think that he had discovered sex and was trying to spread the word single handedly. I had two buddies that I hung around with in those days. He always wanted to tell us about his latest sexual exploit. Neither of us was all that interested. We were able to avoid him by going somewhere else to buy our sodas. But, this was just one guy, at one service station, who didn't stay long. We lived in a small community and could be safe almost anywhere we went. We didn't hear a lot about drugs, sex, alcohol or partying because not many people where we lived did that sort of thing. Some people argue that most of the kids on social networking sites self-monitor the older persons and avoid them like we did the "sex expert" on my block. Social networking sites offer 100 million other ideas about sexual involvement. It's probably true that a lot of the kids de-select some of the more obvious attempts to get them involved in things that are unseemly. But there are plenty that don't and plenty that sneak in. *Once your child has seen pornography or has some sort of heartbreaking experience there is very little you can do to take those impressions away. If you don't believe me, go back and read the experience of Priscilla Dann-Courtney at the beginning of this chapter.*

There is no wonder that there are literally dozens of instances of young women getting into trouble by meeting one of their so called friends in person. Almost any adult can predict that this is going to happen. This adult can tell you that continued exposure to sites that demystify and normalize sexual activity can and often does lead the curious to move on to pornography.

Advice to Kids from an Old Fisherman

There are some things that work a certain way whether or not you are talking about fish or people. Colors are like that. Don't let nobody tell you that animals can't see color – they can and it makes 'em do stuff they wouldn't otherwise do. Animals and people ain't that much different.

Most animals, especially fish, don't have the same brain that you do. But they do have a part of your brain. It's the part that governs instincts, meanness and sex. Most folks call it the "lizard brain" because that's 'bout all most lizards and the like have to work with. When a big mouth bass has already filled his belly and is lazily floating around his favorite hangout you can still hook him if you tickle that part of his brain. Colors like hot pink, chartreuse, baby blue work good for that. If it's late in the day – on toward evening say – something red with some sparkly stuff to catch the light might jog him into biting – just because it's bright. I go down by the beach every once in a while and see little girls in big swim suits and big girls in little ones. The older girls are wearing the same colors that make the fish brain jump into gear when nothing else will.

Girls do the same things to us guys. They will get your attention with a hot pink shirt and earrings that look a whole lot like some spinner baits I got in my tackle box. On toward evening they can put on a red dress and invite you to dance, you can't resist. Take a look at Paris Hilton going into night club some where – she looks like a big top-water lure. Her eyes are highlighted and painted on; she's wearing a little short skirt and a bunch of jewelry that makes her look like a Hawaiian Wiggler. (One of the best bass buster lures every made.)

When a fisherman really wants to get the big old bass brain active, he will make the lure look too good to pass up. You can take just about any ole plug bait and make is swim with its belly exposed. Every animal in the world but one has the good sense to keep their belly covered except when they are hurt or dying. The human female has been exposing her tummy for years – hula dancing, belly dancing and wiggling away for men. The effect is the same for bass or boy – it triggers a response in the lizard brain. I've seen 'em standing around the outside of a dance floor. They got the same wide-mouth look on their face that a bass' got.

If all else fails every tackle box has got a bottle of spray on scent that will make the lure look good and smell good too.

This old fisherman would like to point out something to both boys and girls. It's country wisdom, probably too simple for most folks. Seems like everyone today wants all the answers to be real complicated when they don't need to be. This is one that ain't.

Girls, bright colors, pretty smells and sparkly things will get the attention of boys. But you have to understand that you are appealing to the dumbest part of his brain. The big mouth bass that you attract will not be doing his best thinking. The grey matter is where we make our best decisions. With it we decide what kind of man or woman we will be and develop character, empathy and the ability to make and keep a relationship with someone else. If you have to resort to being "bait" to catch a boy – you spend your life with a big mouth.

Guys, keep this in mind. A girl who only thinks of herself as bait is not going to be much company when things get tough and you need the helping hand of a good woman. Keep in mind; every bait in the tackle box has a hook in it.

Woody Edmiston

Chapter Two

PORNOGRAPHY AND SNS

—⚏—

Hott and Sexy

A large number of the sites on social networking have a sexual undertone or overt sexual content. But that's not where it stops. They are not just for pornography or hot sex talk; they are advertisements for kids to buy products and services. Models on those sites wear low cut pants, bikinis, lingerie or whatever they don't quite have on. When you look closer there are many dating services for young urban professionals. They are sites that charge to put you in touch with the "love of your life." Why they are advertised with slinky, semi-nude women is probably something that their marketing research branch put in place. The point is that you just can't escape sexually drenched material while you are checking out internet sites. Semi-nude models seem to advertise just about everything that is marketed to your children today. Clothing, perfume, body sprays, jewelry; each is sold by sexy models. They are young, attractive people with a look on their faces that says they are *really ready* for something hot and sexy. **Keep in mind that of the roughly 130 million users, at least half are too young to be involved in sex unless that person is a supporter of "childlove."** Childlove is something else that you may not know about. They even have their own logo system. The Childlove Online Media Activism Logo was created as an identifier for online media like blogs, podcasts and webcasts, to promote the idea of youth civil rights and childlove acceptance. It is the "brand" for organizations that promote the idea that sex between children and adults is normal and natural. And their membership uses electronic media too. (*Be real careful* what keywords you use when you try to research this on your computer. You will either get a lot of cookies, adware and similar "Trojans" attached to your hard drive – or you might get a knock on the door and a visit from local law enforcement. WDE)

It would be hard to find anyone outside the Childlove community who does not understand that for adolescent children recognizing one's sexuality is an emotionally difficult period. After years of police work, taking children off of back roads with their pants around their ankles, pulling skinny dippers out of public parks and finding runaways who turn up pregnant a few weeks later, I am pretty clear on the fact that some teens have sex too early. I've also gone to church and sat behind a 14 year old who flashed a hot pink thong over the back of her low cut pants. It made me want to whack the parent next to her in the back of the head with a hymnal. "What were you thinking when you bought those?" Kids not out of high school are not ready for sex and therefore don't need seductive clothing. Children who have not yet mastered algebra and can't be licensed to drive don't need racy underwear. They counter: "Well, I want her to feel good about herself." For what, so she will feel good about trading sex for the elusive ability to be part of "the group?" We lived in a society not too long ago that understood these things.

> Teens that have sex before age 15 face a number of physical and emotional health risks. They are more likely than other teens to have unprotected sex, to have many sexual partners, to be intoxicated while having sex, and to get a sexually transmitted disease (STD). Most young teens are not ready to deal with the emotions that go along with sexual intercourse. Because they are just beginning to learn about emotional intimacy, they are more likely to have sex with someone they do not know well than with a relationship partner. (Morgan 2002)

I am not sure if the above paragraph is a warning to parents or if it is a motivational message for perverts. Read it again and you will see what I mean. WDE

Social networking is primarily about advertising things to the users. It's not just a free altruistic form of public communication. It's intended to be a vehicle that lets the user associate the fun he is having with his friends and the products being advertised. I should tell you that major advertisers are planning to expand on the idea. It will be called a "peer recommendations framework." A PRF allows the advertiser to use your child to positively influence the buying decision of other children. According to the Hollywood Reporter, [3] the only thing they are worried about right now is whether they can do it covertly. They plan on sampling every user and making a determination just what market niche the user fits. Every time your "user" says the word – hotdog or body spray – for instance it will be recorded for marketing purposes. Every purchase is recorded and both purchases and word uses are recorded for future use. Over time "xxjungleluvboy" as he likes to be called, has a detailed buying profile. The words that he uses will be reprocessed and used to send unsolicited emails that he will be enticed to open. Someone will send him an email with the words New Body Spray in the subject line. The actual product they are promoting might be a penny stock or a porn site. These messages are all about consumerism and not much about friends. In fact, if you look at a lot of sites right now you will see that the users are already getting with the program. They are *volunteering* to endorse brands like Abercrombie Fitch, Hollister, Old Navy and similar brands. They list these brands on their sites as a part of their identity. *Which means the advertising is working!*

Buyer profiles

To look a little further into the minds of these advertising types consider that one of the main features of modern marketing is the compilation of buyer profiles. Your child is making of himself a commodity saying, "Here are all my good points, love me, like me, share with me!" The marketing community is working on how to do that. They want to "share" their opinion with your child that he should buy their product. At some time in the future advertisers will be creating online, "cyberfriends." A cyber friend in this case is simply a bit of software that can look at the line of dialogue your child places in an Instant Message and derive some sort of appropriate response.

Imagine your teen sitting down at the computer to do homework. Shortly after logging on, a message screen pops up in the lower right corner of the screen. Your teen is not really excited about doing homework and looks to see that Jiminikrikit "wants to be your friend." Your teen may never realize that Jiminikrikit is not another 15 year old kid, it's a computer. The program takes over the conversation by asking questions.

Yourkid: Hi, Jiminikrikit

Jiminikrikit: Hi, whatsup?

Yourkid: I'm bummed, my homework is really getting out of hand.

Jiminikrikit: Sounds like you need a break!

Yourkid: You bet! I wish I had somewhere to go.

Jiminikrikit: Do you know about, The Fright House?

Yourkid: No, what is it.

Jiminikrikit It's a place on Canal Street, there are lots of good bands and they have armbands for kids underage to get in – but they won't serve you drinks ☹

Yourkid: What bands?

Jiminikrikit: the greatest band I ever heard there was Audio Mayhem – have you seen their new cd –they are all naked on the cover – except they are painted to look like flags?

Yourkid: u gotta be kidding me!

Jiminikrikit: Not kidding. Do u like café latte?

Yourkid: Mmmmm? Yes!

Jiminikrikit : Fright House has the best kaffelatte – that's the way they spell it – in the world. My friend Kevin works behind the bar – he gives me an extra shot of … never mind what he gives me, u may be too young. LOL

Ok, that is enough. This whole conversation, although I just made it up, could easily happen on any SNS that is picked out by a mass adder program. When Peer Recommendations Frameworks are used, his or her site will be chosen because your teen, at some-time in the past, discussed a specific topic, say: night clubs or bands. The mass adder is just advertising a Club. The club lets in teens that are too young to drink, but gives them a colored bracelet to show they shouldn't be served alcohol. There is a suggestion that once they make friends, they can get an extra shot of something in their non-alcoholic drink. They even threw in a few misspellings to make it look authentic. Do you think your kid is more motivated to do their annoying homework following this conversation? Jiminikrikit could just as easily be advertising a tooth whitening toothpaste or a free trip to the Bahamas. In fact, the longer Yourkid maintains the contact with Jiminikrikit the greater the number of products that will be mentioned in their conversations. Someone who has the Jiminikrikit PRF can charge advertisers to blast these out all over the states. Jiminikrikit will work 24 hours a day asking kids all over the world to be their "friend." When he is accepted, he will begin telling them all about the latest and coolest products. It's kind of annoying to me to have the kids at my child's school influencing him. But it is more annoying to think that the "kid" is a computer belonging to a mass merchandiser who is capitalizing on my child's naiveté. Cyber friends will be pre-programmed to talk to your teens on a peer level to encourage them to buy a product. Your child will then recommend or introduce Jiminikrikit to others based on their relationship. One has to assume that this cyber buddy will not be programmed to first check with you to see if the product is some-thing your child really needs.

Fake myspaces

The people selling perfume and clothing are not the only ones that are getting in on the idea of advertising in the social networking arena. The promoters of pornography have already set up phony social networking identities that are overt attempts to get you to spend money. Here is how this works. An adult website has a space set up with a picture of a really gorgeous girl. On its face, it is not identified as an adult site nor does it indicate that it will refer the user to an adult site. It just appears to be a site for a cute girl. Embedded in the site is a Mass Adder program that constantly prowls the internet looking for users who are currently on line and have the right profile. Let's say - male subscriber, 21 to 45 who lives in a particular city. **Keep in mind that age does not have to be proved so your 15 year old may have a profile that says he is 21**, hoping to get into a conversation with an older girl for "bragging rights." (It is common for both boys and girls to fudge a little when claiming their age on SNS.) The program will randomly locate a user and ask to be a "friend" on the social networking site. Her profile looks legitimate but the picture is not of another user. She/he is a part of a scam, probably a model. One of the things she will tell you up front is that she does not like people who don't know how to have fun and won't spend money to do it. The pitch is designed to make the user more willing to use a credit card later. The people who are sophisticated enough to use something as new as a Mass Adder program to lure users to a web site are also smart enough to use mass marketing techniques. They will have used focus groups, professional sampling tools and other marketing techniques to discover just what to say and when to say it. This type of thing is not two weird guys fantasizing in their basement. It's big business.

If your child decides to hit this space with a "friend request" something called an IM Bot or Instant Messenger Robot takes over. It is a program that is created to make your child think he is getting to know a really "hip chick." They begin a conversation that at first seems rather benign. She tells him that she has a special site and is about to go on a live camera. She invites him to take a look. At the last minute she offers special instructions on how to get a VIP pass. Eventually he will be asked for a credit card number. At that point your child, who is probably using one of four fake profile names and *your credit card,* is plugged in to a genuine XXX adult website. He may not make it on the first time because he had not talked you out of a credit card yet. But the IM Bot will continue to hit him with profile after profile after he has shown interest. (http: moneydick.com)

Prediction

As a final prediction, I suggest that this whole area of trust will be also altered by the creation of multiple identities, names and lifestyles. Intrusions of IM bots and PRFs into our children's lives have a great potential to lead people into situations where they can be hurt emotionally and financially. The most important thing a person has is his own good name. What will be the effect on a generation if its members neither know who he/she really is nor can anyone depend on the concrete identity of the other members? More important to you, can your teen develop a truly healthy identity by playing multiple identity roles to tease others into liking them. What does it say about your identity if you have to make up things to be liked?

Normalizing sex at an early age.

We have talked about subscribers to these web sites being bombarded with impressions that normalize sex, glamorize scanty clothing; and glorify steamy romance. Many of the conversations between kids on the sites are just as sexually laced. They make reference to making out or having a significant boyfriend or girlfriend. The kids who pass messages back and fourth send questionnaires that titillate and tease. The following is one of the more tame examples.

Sexy Test

This is the "Sexy" test. Reply through a message with your answers. Post this and see who will fill this out. You may be surprised to see some of the answers.

How old do i look?
[] 14
[] 15
[] 16
[] 17
[] 18
[] 19
[] 20

[] 21
[] 21+

Do you think i have a nice body?
[] yes
[] no
[] can't tell

I am..
[] hott
[] decent
[] sexy
[] ugly
[] cute

I look like..
[] a player
[] a cute girl
[] wifey type
[] one time thing
[] a hottie
[] a husband type

If you saw me for the first time would you talk to me?
[] Yes
[] No

Would you rather..
[] hook up
[] cuddle
[] have sex
[] date
[] make out
[] stay together

Would you like it if i..
[] sang you a song

[] made a shirt with a picture of you on it
[] got a tattoo of your name on my chest or belly
  button area
[] took you out on a romantic night
[] kissed you in the rain
[] danced with you in the rain
[] made love to you and stayed with you because you
  were special to me

On a scale of 1-10 (10 being the highest), rate me..
[] 1
[] 2
[] 3
[] 4
[] 5
[] 6
[] 7
[] 8
[] 9
[] 10

Are you going to repost this so i can answer for
YOU?
[] yes

You should take into consideration that I know the child who posted this list. It doesn't mean that she created the test, only that she re-posted it. She is a sophomore in high school which puts her in the 15-16 year old range. (I deleted all of her answers on the test.) She has two parents, lives in a middle class family and attends church within 10 miles of my home. Go back and look at that checklist. There is a suggestion built in to that list of questions that whomever sent it would accept as a "date" a person who would answer the questions this way: *You look 14, I think you have a hott body and you are sexy, if I met you for the first time I would talk to you, You look like a one time thing but, I would have sex with you, and, I would like it if you made love to me.* The fear I have is that the kids who read these posted and reposted lists will begin to accept this sort of limited expectation of sharing ones feelings, emotions, sexual relations and permanence as normal. Therefore, they are allowing other teens, not you, your pastor, or even their teachers to define an acceptable inter-personal relationship.

Demystifying sexual experience

The following posting was from a boy. I do not know this kid. He stated on his space that he was 17 but his picture does not look like he is much over 12.

A Girls First Time
(Assume you are a girl if you are a boy)

It's your first time. As you lie back your muscles tighten.

You put him off for a while searching for an excuse, but he refuses to be swayed as he approaches you. He asks if you're afraid and you shake your head bravely.

He has had more experience, but it's the first time his finger has found the right place. He probes deeply and you shiver; your body tenses; but he's gentle like he promised he'd be. He looks deeply within your eyes and tells you to trust him - he's done this many times before. His cool smile relaxes you and you open wider to give him more room for an easy entrance. You begin to plead and beg him to hurry, but he slowly takes his time, wanting to cause you as little pain as possible. As he presses closer, going deeper, you feel the tissue give way, pain surges throughout your body and you feel the slight trickle of blood as he continues. He looks at you concerned and asks you if it's too painful. Your eyes are filled with tears but you shake your head and nod for him to go on. He begins going in and out with skill but you are now too numb to feel him within you. After a few moments, you feel something bursting within you and he pulls it out of you, you lay panting, glad to have it over. He looks at you and smiling warmly, tells you, with a chuckle, that you have been his most stubborn yet most rewarding experience.

You smile and thank your dentist. After all, it was your first time to have a tooth pulled.

What were you THINKING?! NAUGHTY!!

Who was the author?

Let's examine Girls First Time. This is obviously a description of sex between an experienced partner and a virginal girl. I don't think this is a description penned by a teenaged boy. This is something that was created and circulated by a much older person for his own perverted vicarious thrill. It is written by someone who seems to be hoping to demystify the first act of sex and encourage young women to have the experience. There are people out there trying to find a teen aged sexual partner. Some of them are 15 some of them are 51. They fantasize that there are girls who would try sex with a stranger (see the above quote - Morgan 2002) for the first time if he promised to be gentle. The sad fact is that there are girls who will. Many girls and boys who are confused about sex and who desire some sort of relationship become desperate. They are so eager to have some sort of connection to another person, that they are willing to try sex with a stranger. Remember this the next time you are letting your daughter select racy underwear.

Intervention

To be fair, most of the networking organizations do offer some advice somewhere on the site about privacy and safety. MySpace says the key is to use "common sense." (We have just spent a lot of time explaining why teens don't yet have common sense; and there is more to come.) The user is warned that the spaces are public and to never give out personal information or their specific whereabouts. Of course, they tell you to never give out your phone number or give out information that would allow a stranger to find you. Equal value is given to safety, avoiding hate speech, avoiding saying things you will regret later and misleading people into thinking you are older than your years. This is presented in a section of the web space that I suspect is seldom if ever visited by the average teen. Of all of the conversations that I have seen and conducted with kids on the sites, none of them have ever mentioned the safety section of a site.

What enforcement action can you expect if you violate any of these rules? If you are a pervert pretending to be eighteen or under when you are not: ***they will delete your account.*** Of course we are referring to the free account that one can create again in about 10 minutes under a different name. It's not a particularly effective intervention.

Not all sites are restricted

The examples of language and objectionable materials in this book were found using my son's site. Many examples are shown in the Appendix of this book. *The site shows him to be sixteen.* There were no barriers to his reaching the so-called personal sites of porn stars, Playboy magazine centerfolds and people willing to talk about the most graphic sexual matters on line. For a teen, just looking at one of these sites without having any instant message exchanges with the user or exchanging photographic materials would be too much, too soon. Once a person gets interested in illicit sex and pornography there seems to be a slippery slope quality that can't be overcome. If users can have this sort of conversation about sex what other less sensitive yet dangerous topics will be discussed?

About pornography

***Warning**: the next four paragraphs contain graphic descriptions of deviate behavior and are the reason children should not be allowed to read this book.*

Every parent has worries that the internet will give their child the opportunity to see porn. I originally had decided to ignore it almost completely in this book because you already know that pornography is a bad thing. However, the more I studied social networking sites the more I realized they are a corridor leading to pornography; as well as other areas that are socially unacceptable — especially for kids. Let me throw my opinion into the mix about this topic. If one looks at how pornography affects a life, the obvious choice is to avoid taking the first steps. Pornography can have long term effect on the ability of a man to keep and establish relationships.

"Once you become addicted to it, and I look at this as a kind of addiction, you look for more potent, more explicit, more graphic kinds of material. Like an addiction, you keep craving something which is harder and gives you a greater sense of excitement, until you reach the point where the pornography only goes so far - that jumping off point where you begin to think maybe actually doing it will give you that which is just beyond reading about it and looking at it." (Dobson, 1995)

The significance of this quote is that it came from an interview with Ted Bundy. He was one of the most notorious and prolific sado-sexual killers in the 20th Century. Shortly before his execution he met with James Dobson a psychologist and author of several books about adolescent behavior and parenting. If you want to learn more you should read his books. Other sources of this quote would be in a stodgy psychological study or a book about serial murders. For an old cop like me – that's good reading. You might not think so.

Bundy did not blame pornography for his crimes. He took full responsibility for them right up to the final interview he gave just before his death. It is important to our discussion because of its rela-tion to identity. Bundy said that the interest that he developed at an early age with pornography changed him — **changed his iden-tity** — and made him desire greater and greater thrills associated with sexual gratification. I have read Bundy's story (Larsen, 1980) and had the opportunity to learn in law enforcement seminars about this behavior from officers (Robert Ressler, Roy Hazelwood) who spent a long time interrogating him and studying his psychological makeup. I have also arrested people as a police officer who were heavily involved in pornography. It is as addictive as any drug and the effects are quite the same. There is an effect that causes the viewer of pornographic materials to seek out progressively more erotic and then weirdly or perversely erotic images. At a point, the users tell me that your inhibitions slip to the point that, especially with the addition of drug use, nothing is taboo.

In the town where I served as police chief, a home disturbance caused our local officers to call for help from other agencies. When they arrived we began to look for three naked men who had been seen running through a trailer park. One of them was armed with a large knife. He had threatened at least one person with it. During the search a person from a neighboring trailer park called asking for help. We found two of the men, brothers is their early twenties, hiding in the closet of the home. They were high on methamphetamine. In that state, they had been in the closet long enough to forget that they were being pursued by police. When the door was opened to the closet, the brothers were simultaneously performing oral sex on each other. When we searched their homes they had two computers that were streaming pornography and they had multiple tapes, books and other types of pornographic materials. When we interviewed them later they claimed no memory of the events of the evening. One of them, a man not yet 30 years of age, confided in me that he had been viewing porn since he was a child and that he could no longer become aroused unless he first looked at pornography. He started watching porn in his own home, with his parent's knowledge. The parents were also methamphetamine users.

The possibility of this young man having a normal life is almost zero. It started when he began to look at pictures using a brain that was not completely developed. So those images were a part of his developmental process. On a very basic level, his identity was that of a pornography devotee. Only a complete change of his life would be possible to overcome that addiction. No amount of porn is OK!

Chapter Three

VULNERABILITY OF ADOLESCENTS AND ADOLESCENCE

—∿—

"Who cares if some lame emo kid offs hiself? (sic) It just frees up space for the rest of us and we don't have to listen to his self absorbed s—t anymore."

A sensitive myspace user

Character and social consciousness are not something that we come equipped with at birth. We are born helpless. I have often said that we are committed by our anatomy to live in a society. Without the help of others we cannot survive. Some wild animals, like the alligator, pop out of the egg shell with all the teeth, claws and armament they need to hunt something down and kill it. They may only be able to kill a cricket, but they can kill and eat. They are able to meet their needs in an animalistic manner. Being humans, we are vulnerable and defenseless for the first several years of our lives. As a result we must live socially; that is with other people. While he is in even the smallest dyad of mother and child, the child begins to learn rules of behavior. Our larger society expects every child to learn its rules and follow them. By a certain age, usually about 13, all societies expect its members to understand the basics and then continue to develop what they have learned as they age. That development or absorption is something called ***internalization,*** a term I will use often in this book. We all want to be able to tolerate your kid at the mall or the supermarket. If each of us teaches our kids to be tolerable then we are all peacefully coexisting. Judging from what I have seen at the mall lately, some of you are getting behind on your job.

While an infant is helpless he is also is the epitome of self gratification. An infant's existence is one impulsive need after another. They have no self-control and they must be taught everything. As they grow older we try to teach them the elements of social responsibility. However, to truly have good character the person must have the desire to be a good person and have self-discipline that comes from within. Much of that inner strength is placed there by good parenting. Good parenting is what puts the desire for decency in a child's heart. A child does not automatically have a conscience. Not only does support for good behavior and decency come from the family it comes from the community. Ideally, the family places emphasis on trust and helps one to develop trust. The members of a small community often perform the same function. The larger the group, the less likely one is to be able to trust everyone in the group. When parents fail at this task and the child reaches the point that he has physical strength, having not internalized the norms of society; he will act in an animalistic fashion. If he is really off track, having never been trained out of the behaviors of the two year old, he may literally hunt something down and kill it. At adolescence, the predatory nature of the child is still close to the surface. I offer the current gang problem in many communities as an example.

Predatory youth

In the case of most youth today, they are already living in a social structure that seeks out any sign of weakness and attacks it with great energy. Of course, the social structure I am speaking of is the typical public school. However, it is commonplace for all children to think that he or she comes from a background/family/small town that is not as normal or real as the other kids that belong to that ideal example of what teen life should be. What I am referring to here is what I mentioned regarding the teachings of Max Weber, renowned sociologist. This is true, regardless of the type of upbringing you have given your child. Adolescent angst is far too commonplace in Junior

High and High School. When it happens for the first time to a child, it is hurtful and memorable. For a child from a broken home or one with a single parent who had a history of injury to his soul, this can be especially painful. Yes, I know that there are a huge number of children being "successfully" raised by a single parent. I was a child raised by a single parent. The felt difference to a child of having an intact family versus anything else is enormous. If you want to argue that there is **none** – try to imagine me with my fingers in my ears saying – blah, blah, blah. Besides, what I said was, "from a broken home . . . or single parent . . . *with a history of injury to his soul.*" That happens when one parent dies, gets a new lover, abandons the family and fails to parent the child or worse, physically harms the child. Since almost every kid identifies his family structure or his experience in it as "different" they will go to almost any extreme to keep their classmates and peers from seeing them that way. Feeling different is tantamount to being different in high school and that is the last thing the child wants. Appearing weak is guaranteed to at least ostracize and most likely to invite the attention of a bully. The average public school is not necessarily a safe and nurturing place; as the SNS message below would indicate:

A myspace warning

> All **freshmen** read this and take it for what it's worth. Congrats....now you're the lowest of the low. Here are just a few helpful words of advice:

> 1) You are NOT cool.
> 2) Everyone DOES Hate You.
> 3) You ARE annoying.
> - Do not wear ripped jeans and an Abercrombie shirt because you want to make "a variety of friends."
> - Do not slick your bangs to your face and wear "bracelets" in you're ears because you think that you're Hood.
> - Sex doesn't make you cool, and if you do have sex don't tell anyone. Nobody cares, really.

59

- You are a F-R-E-S-H-M-A-N.. not a "Freshie".. shut up you sound GAY.
- Don't think you're smart because you filled up water bottles with vodka and snuck it onto your 8th grade field trip. We've all done it.. so don't be proud.
- Don't try the Emo scene. Just don't do it.
- DO NOT think that the upperclass girls/guys are your best friends. They hate you.
- Don't think that you have privacy now that you're in high school. Once you're here, your business is everyone's business, yes there IS still drama, probably even more.
- Don't try to sit at upperclassmen lunch tables. You will be picked up and thrown onto the floor.
- You'll never be as hott as the '07, '08, and '09 people. So don't try!

- DONT TRY TO ACT OLDER THAN YOU REALLY ARE. The way you walk, dress, and talk just has freshman written all over you. That is my FAVORITE one.
- You're "The Class of '10" haha.. enough said.
- If you are black, hispanic, etc. WE GET IT, You love your country! Thats peachy but dont make everything a race related issue because your poo still stinks.
- PLEASE NO MORE XXXXL shirts and ridiculously baggy pants on skinny white kids, nobody likes white chocolate. Allow me to kick you in the face.
- If you are going to try and rebel, it most likely won't work.
- Don't be a slut. This should be the number one rule.

- DO NOT crowd our halls like cattle, because the upper classmen can (& most likely will), push you out of the way. You will get hurt.
- Don't try to get with a boy/girl who's older than you. Chances are, if they are attractive they are taken, & their girlfriend/boyfriend will have no problem f—king you up.
- Don't think your the bomb because you finally passed junior high we all did it it wasnt too hard. But welcome to the hardest years of your life. Welcome to HELL....

Believe me—You can't win. Have fun being a freshman...for a fun-filled year with no life and no opinion whatsoever.

Sincerely,

-The Classes of '07, '08, and '09

Hollywood movies have done a lot to educate our children about College fraternity initiations. For the most part, this sort of thing does not really take place in high schools all that often. Reading this posting (Aug 2006) you can see that the author has circulated this message with the intent of "laying down the law" to underclassmen. She is attempting to enforce a sorority type of pecking order a bit early. This is high school. The teachers are supposed to be in charge aren't they? The writer doesn't think so. Let's take a look at this message. I'll use the author's format:

1. It is vulgar. A lot of what is posted on a social network site uses profane and vulgar language.* So your child is going to learn vulgar language from his social networking space. There is no getting around it. Will they go on to use it? What do you think?
2. The first three lines directly attack the identity of the reader and points out freshmen are valueless. Your

child is going to take it for granted that there is a possibility of being singled out and made to feel like a complete geek.

3. The author establishes himself as an authority, criticizes fashion, hairstyle, and rebuffs any attempt that a new kid would make at trying to be friendly. Keep in mind that if a new freshman is coming from another school they do not know anyone. How is he or she supposed to know who is an upperclassman?

4. There are three direct threats to physically harm the freshman: "upperclassmen can and most likely will push you out of the way. You'll get hurt" and "you will be picked up and thrown to the floor" and still "their older boyfriend/girlfriend will have no problem f—ing you up."

5. There is also the direct inference that bringing alcohol to school is an old and accepted thing and that you shouldn't brag about it because everyone has done it. The writer also seems to indicate that the freshman is coming to school with the expectation that he or she will engage in sex with classmates.

* See the page of myspace acronyms.

Messages of this type are circulated regularly on network sites. This is certainly not the only one; it is just one of the more egregious. Each will be aimed at setting standards of behavior. Not all of them will be this obvious. But the number of them that are on the web sites would probably amaze you. This is rooted in a child's unconscious desire for order and rules. It is at the heart of what is wrong with the way we have been raising our children since the post war period. Children want rules, instructions, and things to believe in. They don't want their parents to just be their friend and help them get in touch with their feelings.

My guess is that most parents are not going to be any more excited about a group of "upperclassmen" deciding what is right and wrong for their child than they are a mass merchandiser. **Why**

do parents need a national distribution center (SNS) for information that is destined to undermine good parenting? Why do we need such a place when that site is not censored or vetted in any manner? Most of us really do believe that there is an ideal type of behavior for most circumstances. We understand the basics of right and wrong. We don't want our children getting their ideas about right and wrong from the "ignorance pool." We want them to internalize a more familiar set of beliefs. We want them to have those we believe in. At home we try to set these standards. But when a peer makes an off handed suggestion that sex is really great in the back seat of a car or that oral or anal sex "doesn't count" it undermines everything you have told them up to that point about the subject.

This is important!

The sort of behavior outlined in the example above has always existed in high schools in some minor way. I understand that there has always been peer pressure. It is important to remember that the people who are corresponding on these sites are peers. What will be the result of a large number of our children reading similar bulletins and corresponding with each other about what they have learned? I think bulletins of this sort and SNS messages will do more to influence them than anything adults say to the contrary. The message gives permission to upper classmen to humiliate your child. What will the next one do?

The Emo or Goth kid

One of the most noticeable personality types online is the Emo or Goth kid. Children drawn into this lifestyle have a tendency to be fixated for a long time. They lose a lot of time that they should be using to prepare for life contemplating their own misery. For those in the know, Emo and Goth are actually two entirely different things. Emo is a short and somewhat derogatory term for a child caught up in his feelings and emotions. On the web sites they are the underclass. In the social work community we would say that they either have a personality disorder or that they were emotionally disturbed. These are children you might remember from grade school who would cry a lot. They get hurt often on the playground and their wounds are primarily psychological. They continue to cry for a long time over a small injury. Many of them have lived in chaotic homes and the damage done there is hard to fix.

To truly be Goth, one is probably a little older than your average high school kid. Gothicism dates to the late 1970's and is a little long in the tooth for a high school group. The real pivotal element of the movement is a form of music that is rather past its prime. The things that set it apart are that it is a true subculture and it is of British origin. The ideology of the Goth involves a dark *mood* inspired by late 19ᵗʰ century romanticism, especially that which swirled around gothic novels of the era. I'm referring to Mary Shelly and Frankenstein. That is: ***Frankenstein; or, The Modern Prometheus*** It was published in 1818 and is representative of Romanticism or Gothic literature. Contrary to whatever movie version you have seen, the novel is actually about man meddling in science and technology. It teaches the lesson that man is ultimately doomed to die as a direct result of what he creates. Man should leave technology alone. It fits the current Goth mindset perfectly. The Goth person revels in dark, mysterious, and morbid imagery that is still carried on in modern horror films. The reason they are often misconstrued as Emo and visa versa is their tendency to wear black and Emos love to wallow in a dark mood. A Goth person is often portrayed with sort of a camp theatricality or self-dramatization in movies and television.

There are examples in the television drama's *Crossing Jordan* in which Steve Valentine plays criminologist: *Nigel;* and Pauley Perrette, who plays forensic specialist *Abby Sciuto* in *NCIS*.

Birds of a feather, flock together
The social networking sites are a place where the Emo can be expressive and find others who "feel" the same way. He or she can find people of a like mind and talk about things in a way on the sites that they could never do in real life. Because of the disaffection they feel with society— the *normy* kids— they don't make friends well. The Emo does not have good eye contact and presents with flat affect; expressionless, and with rigid jawed disinterest. Their sites are full of melancholy poetry and complaints about how rotten the world is to them. Most of these children are really working on the ques-

tion, "Who am I?" Some of them adopt a hair style that allows their bangs to hang down covering one eye. Their style of dress is unisex and they have a lot of arm bands and bracelets. They are a type that in the past would have become a beatnik poet or hippy peacenik. The term "beatnik" was coined by San Francisco humor columnist Herb Caen to describe a person who belonged to Jack Kerouac's *beat generation*. Beatniks were part of the counter culture and saw themselves as non-materialistic and artistic. Hippie Peacenik is a term that morphed out of beatnik to describe the kids who became involved in the counterculture scene that formed around Vietnam War protests. Rather than the dark clothes and neatly trimmed goatee of the beatnik, the Peacenik wore loud, multicolored tie-dye clothing and long hair with a scruffy full beard. Both groups had as a central theme a type of music that allowed them to emote.

On the social networks the Emo finds company and validation. At the same time the Emo may find a very strong and mean spirited revulsion to what they represent. MySpace and others are more about living in the here and now. No one wants to be reminded that there is something bigger and better than hooking up, going to parties and shopping for the latest styles. The Emo is on a quest to find his or her identity. Their conversation tends to be about themselves and the agony they feel in searching for "meaning. Misery loves company and they tend to talk about the meaning of life ad-naseum. Most seem mildly if not clinically depressed. Some of them express a lot destructive thought and suicidal ideation. Like their beatnik and hippie forebears, they draw the ire of other social networking users who are not quite as artistically disposed. But also like the hippies they recruit and offer an alternative home to some participants. Emos have a bully pulpit on SNS and they attract new converts regularly.

> "The emo kid . . . one can equate to the new version of the hippie. Both are defined as a large group of people who all pretty much look the same from a personal expression perspective, are part of a movement that either stands for nothing or accomplishes nothing, and are generally looked down upon by a thinking society. From behind it's often hard to tell "Emo-boy A" from Emo-girl B" because they

probably are identical for the hair, mannerisms and pants style. Imagine a metrosexual style for teens that includes pity-party get-togethers and you are pretty much there."[28]

Teens can go to a social networking site and find friends. They can also go to a website and find an identity like the Emo that in the end is harmful. There is such a large group of users online that whatever is interesting or bugging your child he can find a sympathetic ear. Being enmeshed in a group that emphasizes dark mood and tends to validate their depression is no better than being enmeshed in consumerism and night clubs. The Emo identity is not one that is typically beneficial for the long term psychological and spiritual health of a child. This is just one of the odd-ball "isms" that your child can fall into at school or elsewhere. Yet on the social networking sites it blossoms. He or she can find ample reinforcement for all the misery, self hate, parental hate and confusion about sexual identity. In fact they can build a "cave" for themselves on a site where they can display all of their depressed ideology and blog about the uselessness of life. There are many, many philosophies for life on the internet and most of them are weird.

Adult vs. peer learning

Part of one's upbringing is learning from the conversations with adults, relatives, and our peers. Talking to others and exchanging ideas teaches you peer values. The more one talks to others, in fact *enjoys* talking to others, the more one is likely to learn from his circle of friends. **Children will accept their friend's advice over that of an adult.** This is true even if the advice is substantially the same. At a recent camp for foster children, I was helping a group of children participate in a ropes course. One of them froze half-way up the pole. The adults immediately started to try to coax her up to the next step. She did not move. One of the other children (Cassaundra) stepped out of line and walked to a point where the child on the pole could see her. Cassaundra then started saying the same things that the adults had been saying. This time the girl was encouraged to take the next step. The child trusted her peer over the more experienced and trained adults. This is part of the reason every really good class you took in school was one in which the teacher encouraged group participation. For those of us who knew Cassaundra, this was a major step toward maturity.

However, what has happened in this country in the last few years is an assault on American cultural norms. The adults in our society are no longer as cohesive or as much of one mind as they were in the mid-part of the 20th century. Today they are factionalized beyond the wildest expectation of our parents. There are so many belief systems from Marxism to Vegetarianism that we are losing what you and I might have referred to as the American Way of Life. Some of these belief systems take on the quality of a religion. Veganism, for instance, is either a part of several religions or has been practiced like a religion for a couple of millennia. They are still promoting it as something new on social networking sites.

It is into this cauldron that integrity becomes important. You have, hopefully, taught your child to have excellent qualities and they have internalized those characteristics into wholeness. Being one thing inside and out is to be a person of integrity. One has a creed and inner conscience that balances what is right and wrong. Your child most likely does not have the thinking power to choose right and wrong in the face of peer pressure. They cannot make analysis based on experience. They have not yet had personal successes or failures and retraining that comes from a long life. Each of us should have a set of rules to live by and parents must train by example. The idealistic, fairness motivated teen will not accept the admonition: "Do as I say, not as I do."

That is why organizations like Boys Scouts and Girl Scouts memorize a set of ideal standards for behavior. Scouts like Marines have a tendency to adopt the identity of their organization. That is because they have taken the creed of their organization and made it a part of their lives. Children who lack that kind of training do not have the ability to deal with the more scary parts of life.

Some statistics

A study of five high schools in the Bronx and Brooklyn found that one out of 10 girls was infected with Chlamydia or gonorrhea.[4] Adults 18 to 25 years old have a higher rate of current cocaine use than those in any other age group.[5] Alcohol-related crashes are the second leading cause of teen death. Alcohol use is often linked with teen deaths by drowning, fires, <u>suicide</u> and homicide.[6] Some professionals who have analyzed fatal accidents have hypothesized that many of the deaths attributed to auto accidents, especially single-vehicle accidents, may result from suicidal intent. I should make it clear that these statistics were gathered without calculating any effect of social networking sites if there was any. These sorts of effects tend to be cumulative and the sites may not have yet had a statistically measurable effect. The point I am making with these statistics is to underscore the point that this age group is already vulnerable.

When my son took his life, I went to his computer to see what he had been talking about and with whom. I found that he posted a short note to his friends saying goodbye. By the time I looked at the computer, others who knew him had verified that he was gone. Sitting at the computer I noticed that the on line community was choosing sides. Some of them wanted to blame his girlfriend. That child was fragile emotionally and was in the middle of her own crisis. Regardless how bad I felt, I did not want another parent to feel the same pain I was feeling. With the help of one of Ricky's online friends I created a bulletin to explain that the girl was not at fault. In that bulletin, I made the comment that Ricky had been wounded by the mistreatment of other people. He had always seemed to have a demon sitting on his shoulder reminding him that he was not supposed to get ahead. He had been criticized so much he had difficulty believing that good things were intended for him.

Suicide is painless

Within the next few days I began to get emails from all over the country from kids who felt that they had a demon sitting on their shoulder. I spoke with many boys and girls who were hurting. I spent enough time with them to learn who they trusted and got their promise to discuss how they felt with that person.

- One boy had a long conversation with a parent and reported back that this had been an act of freeing himself. He was amazed that his parents got it!
- Another boy commented on the pain that he read at my horror of having to look upon my son's broken body. He caused an accident that crippled him and had taken other lives. Reading the bulletin convinced him to find a positive way to mend the pain he felt, rather than suicide.
- I got to know a wonderful detective with the Odessa Police Department who saved the life of a boy who asked me to give him advice. During our conversation, I realized that the boy was imminently suicidal. The detective and his mental health detectives found the young man after I convinced him to give me his phone number. He had tried four times in the past to kill himself with drug overdoses.

Since I began my study of social networking I came to understand something else about teens with a deeper appreciation: they have a fascination with death. Adults and adolescents experience depression differently. Depression in adolescents usually involves more social and interpersonal difficulties that lead to self-esteem problems. It is arguable, that adolescence is a continuing state of depression. Adolescents tend to idealize suicide as a **solution** to feeling hopeless. Adults tend to see suicide as a way out following a major trauma. Dramatic behaviors such as aggression and an obsession or fascination with death often accompany adolescent depression. Adolescents looking at suicide from the outside want to romanticize it.

Following my son's death his best friend was sent by his parents (good parents) to live with his grandmother for a few weeks. He was sent with instructions to stay off of internet and myspace sites. Why? Because the girls who knew Ricky and his girlfriend were calling him to discuss the **romance** of his death. "Don't you think what Ricky did was the most romantic thing he could do for his sweetheart?" This is a quote from a teen who could not understand the gravity of the experience.

Adolescents do not have the capacity to understand life and death at this time of their lives. They need to be supervised closely and carefully given a bit more "leash" over time. They feel invulnerable and yet they are still very susceptible to all sorts of influences that can permanently alter their lives. There are developmental and physical reasons for this truth. We will discuss them in the next chapter.

Suicide

The idea of lost love that lasts beyond death has been around since Teen Angel lost her race with the train. In that song, Teen Angel (1960) by Mark Dinning, the singer tells a tale of his jalopy being stalled on a railroad track. He bemoans the fact that his true love ran back to get his high school ring and died in the effort. The basic message is that true love outlasts death.

It is safe to say that the concept of suicide or dying for love is a prevailing theme in the chat sessions. Their questionnaires include: *Would you take a bullet for the one you love? Would you want to die if your girlfriend/boyfriend were diagnosed with cancer?* Their teen angst has a tendency to make suicide a real alternative to putting up with the pain of being a teenager. The more they obsess about it and do not get help, the more likely they are attempt suicide. The kids who corresponded with me just needed someone to talk to who was not judgmental; someone who would take what they were saying seriously. I applaud the National Suicide Hotline for having established a presence on MySpace where kids can call and talk about those feelings. [7] Teens can become so desperate to get attention to their pain that they do unexpected and dangerous things to get attention. They cut themselves, throw tantrums, and skip school and other things that many parents cannot see as a cry for help. Instead they see it as defying authority. Getting a child past the point of adolescence sometimes takes a lot of finesse. But you can't finesse anything if you don't have a relationship with the child. If all you ever do is punish your child, you cannot develop a relationship.

I have mentioned this because every one of the disturbed children that I talked to after Ricky's death felt they could not talk to their parents. A parent cannot wait until his teen has problems to try to teach him about right and wrong. In the case of the children that I talked to on these spaces, they had no connection to their parents. At best they had a relationship with a teacher or church leader. One boy told me the only adult he respected was his karate coach. You cannot effect a change in anyone unless you have a relationship with them. From my experience, even that does not work all of the time. There are over 130,000,000 users on MySpace. My little bulletin caused close to twenty kids in my sons small circle of friends to respond. That indicates that there is an enormous number of hurting kids across this country. They are out there experimenting on social networking sites hoping to make some sense out of life.

Unless you, dear parent, establish and maintain a relationship with your children, there is a possibility that they will develop a habit of pleasure seeking that usually ends in tragedy. The people that want to encourage your teen to be involved in the scene don't pretend to have answers. They just exploit the notion that being a part of the action is tantamount to living a life. The general impression is that being a member of this group and building a life full of friends chosen randomly from cyberspace is the equivalent of building a life somewhere else. It is not quality that counts, it's numbers. It's about the people that will pool their ignorance with yours and praise you for decisions about clothing, makeup, hair and accessory, e.g. your look! They will share their music and their poetry with you and tell you secret things about themselves. This is living. This is life. But it has no substance. It only exists in the imagination and the magical thinking of the participants.

Everything about the social networking sites supports and encourages those things that you have taught your children to avoid. It tears down the training and beliefs that you have instilled through countless learning opportunities as they have grown older. Now, as they get to the age that they are about to jump off into adult-hood, these sites offer tantalizing ideas that serve to debunk parental values. SNS derived peer pressure can result in ignorance pooling that leads to stupid choices.

Chapter Five

HOW CHILDREN DEVELOP AND WHY SOCIAL NETWORKING AFFECTS DEVELOPMENT

—⁓—

Theories and practicalities

Children are shaped by their experiences in life. Sociologist B.F. Skinner put forth the theory that an individual's personality is a result of interaction with their environment. The so called founder of psychology, Sigmund Freud, thought that the unconscious mind and childhood experiences greatly influenced personality development. Abraham Maslow theorized there was a hierarchy of needs in human development and if the first four: physiological needs, safety needs, love and belonging, and the need for self esteem were not met; a person could not reach a self actualized state. The point is that every person, every child, develops similarly. Although the theories differ as to how that is done, every child is influenced by the things that happen to him in his childhood. This means every child not just the ones who have crappy childhoods. I like to think of it as wet cement.

Your young child's life is like a layer of wet cement in which other people are constantly trying to scratch their initials. If a soft drink manufacturer gets their initials in the cement early, your child will choose that soft drink for the rest of his or her life. The battle for the opportunity to "initial" your child's mind is one that advertisers, porn producers, television producers and many more, strategize over daily. Advertisers today have identified and segmented every part of the market including the youngest age groups. You have a lot of competition. Your job as parent is to form the concrete, reinforce it with the steel that comes from having character and watch it carefully until it solidifies without someone else defacing it for you.

Societal definitions

Societies define themselves culturally by the way they pass on their rules and their societal knowledge through mores, values and folkways. We know that all mores, values and folkways are definitions. Deviating from those rules or definitions is either a social faux pas or a crime. (Robertson, 1987) Max Weber taught us that whatever a person is doing he assumes that there is an ideal-type of that activity. Weber said that this was a social phenomenon natural to humans. In the case of teens and adolescents, social networks – electronic or otherwise – define ideal activity. What is valid as a social norm is very important in the teen's circle of friends. That is why your reluctance to buy a certain type of skirt or the latest basketball shoes can become a cause for histrionics.

Teens also place a very high importance on fairness. They tend to expand fairness to cover those things they want indiscriminately. It is not fair that someone else has the new skirt and they do not. While an adult is able to understand that there is no imperative for everything to be fair, the adolescent demands it. When you combine the two, ideal activity and a need for absolute fairness, there is opportunity for what social scientists call dissonance. The adolescent misunderstands how life works because his expectation is based in part on errors in thinking.

This tendency toward defining the ideal causes societal confusion because so much is relative even when there are rules. The teenager just does not have the training and experience to know the difference. What we don't know right now is what affect a network site that has the effect of defining values and mores for our children will have in the long term. The same idea was expressed earlier in the quote from Bryn Mawr. What I fear is that these values will be more readily accepted by our children than those held by their parents. This is especially true when those values are taught through questionnaires that only appear to be a fun pastime. In this setting however, they act as teaching tools for a teenaged society. Perhaps the biggest problem is that there are just too many choices. In general the access to these other opinions will have the effect of diluting the importance of local and family norms. [8]

Adolescence.

During adolescence boys and girls are just beginning to form their identities. (Boeree, 2005) They are just learning about romance and intimacy and they are trying to be more self-reliant. At this point they begin to develop their own value system. Adolescent children are very ego-centric or focused on themselves. They feel that no one could possibly understand how they are thinking and resist any suggestion that "we were children once too" from their parents. This is a process called the ***personal fable***, meaning: my experiences are unique. Most adolescents are convinced that they are special and without predicate. This belief is so strong that they think none of life's difficulties or problems will affect them regardless of their behavior. To maintain a perfect life and be indestructible they may create fictitious worlds in which they thrive. Imagine a teen that has trouble having friends or getting a date. They might react by creating a perfect soul mate with whom they are madly in love; that just happens to live in the next state. This is the personal fable; it is a process that is a function of individuation. All teens feel invulnerable (boys even more so than girls) and they cannot accept the notion that their life script is not unique.

Identity Creation.

So far I have talked a lot about how a social networking site becomes a tool for creating identity. Identity creation is extremely important for kids. It should be done with the help of parents and significant adults. Whether they realize it or not a lot of the values the adopt in life were taught years before when they were much younger. Let me explain what I mean with an example.

First, let me explain something about my lovely wife who was raised in a two parent, well structured home with five brothers and sisters. With eight people around the table the winter session and a round of sniffles could make the dinner table a pretty disgusting place to be if the kids had not been taught good manners. In my wife's childhood home, if you needed to blow your nose you went to the bathroom. It was just a way of coping with a large family. It's not a bad habit to get into. Most of my family was made up of dirt farmers and cattlemen. We were happy if the guy with the sniffles used a hanky.

When my son was about 14 he had a real meltdown with his mom over homework. He had become so worked up that he was crying, tears were rolling and his nose was running. We were trying to have a conversation about homework but he could not stop sniffling. He sat there telling me that as soon as he was old enough he was getting away from his mom. She just had too many rules, he hated all the rules and he wasn't going to live his life by rules. "Rules were (sniff) stupid, (sniff) stupid, (sniff) stupid." At that point I handed him a tissue and asked him to blow his nose. *He got up and walked into the bathroom.* He reacted to an internalized rule that his mom, the lady with all the rules; the one he was so anxious to get away from, had taught him years before. He knew that I would not have said anything about him blowing his nose in front of me. But the bathroom rule had become his rule. It was a part of his identity. The irony was so thick I had to stifle a laugh.

When my son went onto social networking sites his identity was still forming. It did not take him long to start questioning some other ideas we had taught him. The first I noticed was his willingness to use foul language. At a later time he decided to begin playing a role on his SNS of someone named Rick Rokr. It became an alter ego. When he found out that he could construct a separate life on his space he became completely immersed in that reality. He began to deconstruct the identity elements he learned from us and replace them with new ones.

When kids have the support of their parents and their community they can create the person that they dream of being or hope to become. On an SNS they can create a personality and a "look" for themselves. When they put their information on their site what they hope for is constructive criticism and praise. Ideally, they **should** get constructive criticism of their sites without any harm being done. That would allow them to improve and develop. From that feedback they could decide which characteristics they would choose to adopt for life. But, if they spend too much time with the Emo they are going to spend a lot of time worrying about imagined slights and focused on feelings. The Scenster is going to teach that personal pleasure, cool clothes and pretty people are all that is important.

Since most of the sites use pseudonyms, it is possible for someone to have more than one online identity. Your budding scenster can be attacked from the anonymous site of a fellow user. One of the things that will be attacked first is parental ideals. From that safe and anonymous spot another user can criticize or bombast your child in the most ugly manner. You don't want your child to be the recipient of such behavior and you certainly don't want your child to behave in that manner. The opportunity for both is ever present. What is worse for parents is the fact that they are not only using it to create their own identity, they are using it to create group identity.

Group Identity

It does not take long before the users develop a **group identity.** They have sub-group names that identify themselves as a person who communicates with his friends on MySpace or another social networking site. They stick together and they have adult supporters. When my son got very involved in computer communication I discussed trying to limit his time on the computer with his computer science teacher at school. I was chastised for not understanding the social importance of chatting with his friends on line. This was from an adult my age so I backed off.

When one begins to form group identity we do so in relationship to other groups. Most of us either see ourselves defined by an occupation or by an avocation. I may be a law enforcement officer by training, but I see myself as a part teacher, part stand up comedian. If I were a doctor I might insist that you call me Doctor Edmiston. Users of social networking sites frequently adopt group identities like Emo Kid, Goth Kid and Normy Kid. Much of the identity formation is also based around music and playing instruments. As a Goth guitar player, a teen might see himself on the way to a career with a heavy metal band. This is how you get rich selling tons of records and meeting pretty girls. (It is, isn't it?) Being a part of a group creates acceptance and validation of beliefs. Each group member then compares himself to other groups seeking status. If we feel better than group X we have greater status. If we feel less status than group Y we might feel somewhat isolated. In the case of the Emo Kid, being defined as an underdog is preferable to being defined as a "rich kid." While bathing in this pool, one should have a very well developed identity to remain an individual. Since most adolescents have not discovered their identity it's easy to adopt the group identity and to internalize it as their own. It is a universal struggle for adolescents to cement their identity and having help from a group is comforting and seductive.

In the process of comparing ourselves, we are compelled to attain status symbols or symbols of group identity that help to reinforce our identity. This is why the advertisers and promoters of social networking sites are just delighted to provide instructions. Those instructions come in the form of advertising ways to dress, wear our hair, and the jewelry and accoutrements of our group. When an adult makes the mistake of questioning the validity of some part of that identity it is liable to cause a response like the SNS user who said: ".give ur children some space no wonder they hate u… do u feel stupid yet?"

Individuation

When any child gets to a certain age he begins to want to separate himself from his family. It is a process called *individuation*, which is: *the process by which individuals in society become differentiated from one another* [9] This process is full of pitfalls and perils.

The process was first synthesized by the famous psychologist Carl Gustav Jung. He said we become self-aware when we discover our true, inner self. Jung supplied specific terminology to the process whereby people throughout history have asked: "Who am I".

Ego: The ego gives you a sense of uniqueness and allows you to differentiate yourself from others. It is what you are referring to when you use personal pronouns e.g. "I am"

Conscious and unconscious: We consciously experience everyday life. The unconscious remains in the background and is composed of hidden aspects of ourselves. It continues to work on the conscious and influence our behavior and actions. These unconscious tendencies can be stronger than our conscious, and can even go against our will. Thus we erupt in anger and yet are very sorry afterwards. The pain and rage we see in children who have been removed from their homes as a result of abuse and neglect, lives in the unconscious. It flares up quite often leaving the foster parents struggling to understand what triggered it.

The Self: The Self is often confused with the ego. The ego is only a temporary structure that gives us an identity in this life. The Self is what we are in *essence*. In psychological terms, it encompasses the conscious, the unconscious, and the ego. (Freud, S, 1923, Jung, C.G. 1945)

Individuation means that one becomes a person, an individual, a totally integrated personality. It is a process of self realization during which one integrates those contents of the psyche that have the ability to become conscious. It is a search for totality. Individuation is a natural, inherent process in man. It cannot be stimulated by something external, it grows from the inside. Just as the body can become deformed, the personality can be deformed by lack of experience, the wrong kind of experiences, and lack of education or education in areas that are not age appropriate. This is why the adolescent is vulnerable to what he or she sees and hears on the internet, social networking and any other mass communication medium.

People Are Watching

Yet another factor in adolescence is the belief that <u>everyone is always watching and evaluating them.</u> They live in fear of being embarrassed by their own actions. They believe they are constantly being judged by members of the group they want to join. That may mean the world of adults or the sorority they want to join. Actually, teens have good justification for this belief. Good parents do watch and judge their children. When they are very little it is important that we judge their actions and correct them. Some parents are still too judgmental at a time when teens should be starting to develop adult lives; hence the fact teens typically clash with their parents over these matters. Parents want to try to see that their children conform to the lifestyle taught them at home. At the same time, teens are trying to learn the rules for whatever group they are trying to join. Those rules relate to us and we are **OLD**. Old is bad. They like the rules they see as young new rules. This is what makes social networking sites so attractive for this age group, it is new. They get to try out ideas about hair and style with less risk of embarrassment. The sites offer a way of beta testing things before they try them out in front of the group. In my opinion this is why SNS and MySpace in particular seems to be made to order for the adolescent.

Previously I said that the tendency toward defining the ideal causes societal confusion because so much is relative even when there are rules. The teenager just does not have the training and experience to know the difference. What we don't know right now is what effect a network site that seeks to define values and mores for our children will have long term. Will these values be more accepted by our children than those held by their parents? In general the access to these other opinions will have the effect of diluting the importance of local and family norms. **In the mean time, they will give your kid ammunition to argue with you!**

Adolescent Antics

It is that period "where bra and funny papers meet"; where bicycles give way to drivers licenses. The adolescent child still has an ability to think in magical terms. The female child can create a "reality" in which she truly believes that she can be the proper parent to a child of her own. About 20% of unplanned or accidental pregnancies with teen girls happen because of lack of attachment and conflict with the girl's parents. **Attachment** is synonymous with the word bonding. Lack of attachment occurs when there is a lack of a relationship with the parent and teen which leads to an inability to have lasting, loving relationships. Children who fail to attach to parents and have the inability to relate to others often do not develop a sense of conscience. It is part of the age-old clash between adolescents and parents. Teens want independence and yet they are still unavoidably dependent upon their parents. In an effort to separate themselves from their families, young emotionally driven girls look for was to differentiate themselves. They feel that having a baby will guarantee having someone to love them and they will have someone to love. (10) Acting on those feelings has given rise to a whole generation of children within the last two decades that bear oddly spelled and imaginatively wrought names like, Laquitha and Jorja. Little girls, barely in their teens, give their babies names like children of post-depression parents named their puppies.

Adolescent boys without parental love and nurturance throw themselves into gangs in hopes of finding structure and a set of rules for living. In the name of "defending their turf" they willingly commit murder and devote themselves to a world where walking on the wrong sidewalk while wearing a certain color is a violation of a gang code of law. During adolescence most boys do not think that adults can help them. Seeking adult help with a problem is to *appear* weak. Boys feel they have to put up a façade. For them appearance is more important than substance. They refer to it as "representing" in gang slang. They rely on each other and tell their friends: "I got your back" as if they were entering a war zone. A few years back, my children and I were in a mall and saw a boy with spiked hair, several body parts were pierced and he had on huge boots and a black leather jacket. He looked scary. The fact is that the child who looked so dangerous was quite likely the most emotionally fragile person in the mall. The children that choose to dress in this fashion are afraid of contact, connection and interpersonal relationships. They fear failing to be socially accepted and present this sort of façade to keep others at a distance. Certainly, these types of children are capable of violence. But their appearance is a result of their own fear. When they do choose to relate to other people it will be only to those who are similarly attired. That means people who dress alike in the manner of the group. They will look to group members by their "uniform" and choose ones who will not criticize. Even in the sub-group that chooses to look grubby, the members will evaluate the "grubbiness" to determine acceptance. You have to look grubby the "right" way. That is because appearance is still all important to one's closest circle of peers.

This is important!

Adolescents have no experiential "database" to draw upon. Making a critical analysis of what they see on social networking sites and life requires more knowledge and life experience than most possess. They simply have not learned enough to determine if the new information and ideas have merit. At the same time, magical thinking allows them to believe fervently in ideas that are contradictory. An example of this might be wearing a lucky charm while driving at high speed believing that it will prevent getting into a wreck. Magical thinking allows the gambler to believe that he is "on a roll" and will continue to win until he changes socks. The point is that teens lack the tools they need to be successful at this time. Without strong parental guidance, good intervention from teachers, preachers and professionals, adolescents can get off track. Getting guidance from the ignorance pool (which is their circle of friends) is not predictive of a good life.

Keep in mind that part of identity creation is the selection of one's sexual orientation. There is a huge debate raging about whether sexual preference is something that a child is born with or whether it is something he or she selects. You should understand that both lesbian and homosexual interests are promoted on SNS as if they were promoting a new deodorant. If your child is trying to create his identity and sexual themes are presented to him or her in such a way that they would solve a problem they might give it a try: e.g. I can't get a date to the prom, I must be gay! Maybe I'll give it a try.

It is good to make mistakes

The reason children play games is so they will make mistakes. That is why we teach ABC's with songs and we use games like Simon Sez to improve memory and mental agility. There will always be mistakes in Simon Say's because of distractions. Therefore it teaches focus. In building teamwork, we use ropes courses and similar games to learn to work together even when mistakes happen. In scouting these are called "teaching opportunities." These games help us teach character. A child will not naturally find a way of developing character. We teach them through learning opportunities that allow us to make safe mistakes. During those games adults have the opportunity to teach fairness and to teach them that winning is a group activity. We teach them that cheating is improper. They learn the rewards of winning without breaking rules. They learn that there is fulfillment by doing things in such a way that it is not harmful to others.

Physiological effects

Have you noticed that your son or daughter seems tense or "wound up" after they have been on the computer for some time? It's because the screens affect them physically. Have you ever wondered about how long is too long to let them watch television? It's probably a lot less than you think. Physical reactions take place while you are facing a television or computer screen because of how the brain and body work. There are, more exactly, *bad* physiological effects caused by computer and television screens. Although your television screen appears to be a steady picture, it is not. You see what you see because thousands of times a second tiny flashes blur together to fool the eye into seeing a single picture. While this might be OK in small doses, it becomes more of a problem when the user spends hours in front of a screen. Users come away from the screen grumpy, stressed and tired.

The reason for this is that the flashes trigger a part of the brain that is tied to the "fight/flight" response. This is also called the **acute stress response.** The more familiar term – fight-or-flight was coined in 1915 by Walter Cannon a researcher in the area of animal behavior. The term was used to describe the reaction an animal or human has when they are threatened or when they are faced with a dangerous situation. This response is created when being frightened causes a sudden increase of adrenaline that stimulates the sympathetic nervous system. This is the part of the brain sometimes called the lizard brain. This is the autonomic nervous system, a sub-system of the central nervous system. It is the part of the brain that is not consciously controlled. When the wildebeest sees the lion sneaking up on him in the African plains, his brain secretes adrenaline and stimulates a response. That allows him to be very efficient at eluding or fighting the lion. The response triggers the following actions:

- The heart and lungs begin to operate faster
- The digestive system slows down
- Blood flow to certain parts of the body change due to constriction of blood vessels.
- Energy is released into the muscles and blood flow is increased to them.
- The pupils dilate and the tear and saliva glands slow down drastically.
- In some cases the bladder or sphincter muscles relax.

A flashing computer screen stimulates adrenaline to flow into the system causing all of these things to occur. Since humans rarely have a need to jump and run from the computer screen we seldom need all this preparation for emergency response. It is there none-the-less. While our body needs this mechanism for self-preservation, prolonged computer use creates a stress response that results in deleterious reactions. The long term effects take a toll on the body and the brain. It can result in suppression of the immune system, panic disorder and trigger post-traumatic stress responses.

The most likely result is that when your teen finally does leave the computer he is grouchy and irritable. He may have trouble sleeping. One of the things I have noticed about the kids that spend lot of time on social networking sites is that they all seem to stay awake until 3 and 4 in the morning. When they talk about it they tell me that they don't need that much sleep. This is rubbish! A developing brain needs 8 hours of sleep each night. It is not even arguable. A teen's brain is still developing and it needs sleep to do so properly.

Find out more about this at www.braingym.org Brain Gym is a program of physical movements that enhance learning and performance. Brain Gym includes 26 targeted activities that integrate body and mind to bring about rapid and often dramatic improvements in: concentration, memory, reading, writing, organizing, listening, physical coordination, and more.

This is important!

Most people don't realize that their **child's brain is still developing** and growing until he or she is **25 years old**. [11] The frontal lobes are the last to fully develop. It is this portion of the brain that does critical thinking. Therefore, children are simply not yet fully equipped to do serious thinking. It accounts for their impulsivity, tendency toward being constantly active and thrill seeking. Most of us are aware that kids tend to think differently or less well than adults. But few of us understand how old a child has to be before he is actually equipped to do serious thinking like an adult.

My cynical doctor friend made the comment that this accounts for why we are able to send teens to war. And he is right! This age is one that is able to be quickly and easily manipulated into a new thinking style. Moreover, this is why you see tiny little boys in third world countries holding Kalashnikov rifles as part of some militia group. They all have an intense expression on their faces that looks out of place on one so young. Young people can be influenced to take a very emotional stand on a political or societal issue. We are learning in the War on Terror that children make very effective suicide bombers because they do not have a fully developed sense of death. They will take several sticks of dynamite into a crowded restaurant because they are told to do it. They don't have the critical thinking skills to argue against an older, wiser authority figure. If they are fully invested in the beliefs of "the cause" they do not want to argue anyhow.

Too much information!

One of the sad facts of social networking spaces is that many children going through personal crisis put their most intimate thoughts on their spaces. This can mean simply goofy thoughts or thoughts ranging from suicide to murder. They may reveal details that, if viewed by certain persons would be embarrassing. How long will it be before the Human Resources departments and College Entry Boards will be scanning your child's comments on his or her social networking site. It will allow them to peer deeply into an applicant's background in a new way. Even though they might be reading information that was posted as a joke or during an emotional low point, it could be used to eliminate them from consideration. [12] I mentioned this in passing to a co-worker. She promptly told me that an acquaintance of hers was fired when someone checked her Xanga account while she was out of the office. They read her bulletin that said she was planning to be out on Friday. She called in sick Friday. Her bosses took a dim view of being told a lie about her absence.

It just ain't so

When a child enters a social networking site and/or the internet they are suddenly exposed to one of the world's larger pools of ignorance swirling with half truths, falsehoods and outright propaganda. They enter MySpace or Xanga et al with the expectation that this site is supposed to help them make friends. They go on the internet expecting to find absolute truth. Most parents think it is a safe place for their child to expand his or her universe while safely sitting at home. Dick Army (US Senator Texas) made the observation that Washington D.C. is full of people who are absolute experts on things that just ain't so! Well from my vantage point, most parents in America today are counting on things in cyberspace to be comparable to their experiences when they were growing up. By now I hope you can see, it just ain't so!

When children this age are placed in a peer group they have a tendency to do what I have been telling you is "pooling their ignorance." Teachers in grades 7 through 12 experience this sort of thing all the time. The peer group will adopt some belief that adults cannot persuade their students to change. One weird example is the belief that taking birth control pills will keep a person from contracting the AIDS virus. Another is that spider eggs in candy actually hatched inside some child's stomach. The spiders then supposedly made their way to his head and "ate his brain." Jan Van Brunvand, who is a professor at the University of Utah coined the term Urban Legend many years ago. The popular television show, Mythbusters, spends a good deal of time and advertisers money debunking legends kept alive by this sort of "ignorance pooling." Social networking sites are rife with examples. Your adolescent child can and will make changes in opinions and make life altering decisions based on this garbage.

Kids are poorly equipped for some tasks

You now know that prolonged exposure to a flashing screen can put them in a mood that is not conducive to your having an open minded heart-to-heart talk. Whatever they have found on the sites is *their* new knowledge and unless you have a good relationship with your child he or she is not going to discuss it with you. And! Since you have learned that your child's brain is still growing and not yet fully functional you should come to two conclusions. Whatever challenges their beliefs on a social networking site – your child is examining it with an *incompletely finished thinking tool*. It is at this age the brain is still very susceptible to influences. Because of that, most parents usually choose to carefully monitor how their child is spending time and with whom. You want to know the parents in the home where your children are spending the night. You don't let them date until they are old enough to handle it. You choose families as your friends that have similar values and interests in order to have the help of those parents to reinforce the values that you want your child to learn. But if you let them stay on the computer for long periods you are opening up channels of communication that may significantly change their thinking and attitude. It may have physical effects that change the way you are able to communicate with your child.

SNS Identity Disorder

I believe that Social Networking Sites (SNS) have the ability to create a disorder in the formation of identity. Kids lost in a world separate from and unmonitored or modified by parental input, can become depressed and less social. A characteristic of adolescent behavior is to retreat to a room or some place that separates them from their parents. It is that part of beginning to individuate. While in that room they will look at themselves in the mirror to find those flaws they think they have. They will compare their looks, their history and their personal fable to what they think is "right" according to what they have learned from peer interaction. What they learn on SNS will only increase their chance of making a goofy decision. They will mull these things over time and time again. Studies have shown that rumination has a deleterious affect on adolescents with Major Depressive Disorder. (Park, Goodyear, and Teasdale 2004) It stands to reason that too much mulling over of anything without some distraction is not a good thing. You know this intuitively. How many times have you had to tell your teen to get out of her room or away from his computer and do something else? While there, in that imaginary space they can make life changing decisions and you know that making decisions in a depressed state is not good.

Although the possibility exists that they will seek out these things anyway social networking sites offer a **heretofore unknown and ominous gateway.** I did not understand the potential for harm as I took a blasé attitude toward my son's involvement. I believe a disorder in personality creation, where he became too involved in an imaginary world, caused my son's death. Further examination of the topic will not bring him back, but I believe it is warranted by his story and other anecdotal information that supports the notion that there is a SNS Identity Disorder.

Chapter Five

THE CULTURAL IMPACT OF SOCIAL NETWORKING

—⟊⟊—

Social networking is a cultural phenomenon

The phenomenon of online communication puts a new burden on children and parents. The burden for the child is to be a part of a scene while the parent is tasked with protecting the kiddo from the dangers that exist. The computer has become so universally accepted as a teaching tool that almost every home has one. Parents take that step specifically to make sure that they provide their child with a chance at success or simply to give them something to do other than television. You should already be familiar with the difficulty some parents have experienced with keeping kids away from pornography and similar sites. Pornography has lead many immature men to become so involved with porn or online affairs that they have left their children behind. This is not new, and it is not the subject of this book, but it is a fact of our culture. If computers have already caused problems in the family, **these sites will only make things worse.** Online messaging appears only to be the latest fad in a long line of fads.

After I began writing this book, an incident occurred in Canada that is indicative of the dangers of the more outrageous effects of this phenomenon. Kimveer Gill, a 25-year-old man from a Montreal went on a shooting spree at a local college, killing one woman and wounding 19 other people. He had an obsession with guns and death, according to his online journal. Kimveer Gill dressed in Goth attire and adopted the name "Trench" a name derived from the ubiquitous Goth trench coats that seem to be part of their group identity. Gill said his credo was: "Live fast, die young and leave a mutilated corpse." On a site called, **www.vampirefreaks.com**, he said that he loved guns and hated people. One of the pictures on his site has the caption "Anger and hatred simmers within me." It is obvious to me, that the site allowed him a place to construct a scheme and rationalize his rampage. Gill was well past the chronological age of adolescence but he was stuck in that state of mind. He had been a victim of bullies, spent hours playing violent video games like Super Columbine Massacre RPG and acting out murders and mayhem while thinking of revenge. In doing so he desensitized himself to the violent acts and practiced motor skills he needed to pull it off. During his deepening depression he went onto his social networking site. There he validated his ideology and found like minded people to talk about his hatred. In the process he created a "hard copy" of the operational blueprint of what he had in mind.

Bullies

There are many people in education that are very disturbed because they believe that schoolyard "bullies" have caused incidents like the Columbine shootings and those in Arkansas. Gill was fascinated by the shooters Dylan Klebold, Eric Harris and everything about the shooting incident. According to an article written by Peter Goldiner in the New York Times, the Super Columbine Massacre RPG [13] game had been downloaded *only* (!?) 40,000 times in the year after it's introduction. (*Check out the description of this game in the endnotes!*) Within a few days after Gill's shooting rampage new users flocked to the SCM RPG site. Another 10,000 downloads occurred in a matter of days. Does this mean there are 50,000 disturbed boys incubating on the social networking sites? Are they engaging in operant conditioning on the Massacre website destined to become killers? As the users worlds intersect, will this number continue to grow? No one knows!

But, we do know something about operant conditioning!

Operant Conditioning

The most familiar type of operant conditioning is the school house fire drill. If they are done frequently, the children will line up and file out of school right way. Once the children are fully trained they will still file out properly even though there is a real fire and they can see flame and smell smoke.

The US military uses video stimulus/response simulators similar to your children's video games. They do this to break down barriers that are taught by parents, teachers and preachers about the sanctity of life. In World War II many of our soldiers had trouble firing at real people because they had trained on circular bulls eye targets. The military in later years began to use pop-up targets (stimulus) of human cutouts to condition the soldiers into the thought of shooting at people (response). The FBI uses Hogan's Alley to teach "shoot-no shoot" techniques with pop-up humanoid targets that either represent gunmen or civilians carrying groceries. Having spent many years as a police officer I can attest to the fact that the stimulus/response activity made me a better and more "thoughtful" shooter.

The FBI agent usually is at least 25 years old and has a college degree. The soldier is at least 18 and is simultaneously trained to have character and to follow rules of engagement. They have thinking skills, training and character controlling their shooting activity. A child playing a video game that allows him to kill and maim has neither.

Social scientists and educators have been working overtime to figure out a way to deal with bullies and social pressures that they say produce shooters like Klebold, Harris and Gill. My guess is that social networking sites are eventually going to be blamed for similar incidents. In fact the inference is clear, in the case of Gill, that the site allowed him a place to internalize his beliefs and plan a course of action. Young people who pull off this sort of thing are ones who have had their identity threatened or discounted by their peers. We hear the psychologists who are interviewed following one of these incidents say that one of the motivators for creating this sort of havoc is to be **remembered**. *I would like to point out that "remembered" is past tense. The implication being that the person "plans" to end his life by being more outrageous than the last guy. The inescapable* *conclusion is that this is a precursor to suicide. Suicide is something that is constantly being discussed on myspace sites. Where does he find out about the last guy who started shooting: the internet, of course?*

The shooters want to be remembered as the person who got even. They want to be baddest of the bad, even if it was for something foul. Kimveer Gill said on his site that he would be remembered as the "angel of death." Young men get this way because children pick on children and adults either don't know or discount what is going on. Had there been a mechanism in place for recognizing what was going on in this instance many lives might have remained unchanged. Kimveer Gill's site was a not just an indication of what might happen. It was a scream! If he had made the same remarks out loud on the corner of any city street, he would have been taken into custody. He would have been charged with Disturbing the Peace, Terroristic Threats or at minimum committed to the local behavioral health center for mental evaluation.

This is important!

Age groups collide on SNS in ways they do not normally. The original reason for an SNS was to expand the network of available dating candidates and find like minded people to share interests of older young people. Rock climbers, rock and rollers, and those who were merely interested in being a part of the Scene flocked to these sites. With the advent of MySpace, teens who want to participate in the Scene, if only vicariously, have their opportunity. Many more social networking sites have come along since. Some of these sites offer spaces for teens to share ideas and be uninterrupted. Since most of physical places in an adolescent's world are actually places that are controlled by adults; an SNS is a haven. But to your child, this digital area is exactly what it was labeled - my space. It is advertised as a way for kids to communicate with kids. *By the way they don't think they are kids anymore.* In no time at all it has become a place where identities are uncertain. Teens, twenty's, thirty's and older all have to opportunity to intersect. Years ago we had places to hang out in public. We went to drive-ins like K& N Root Beer and Dairy Queen. There were roller rinks and parks. Smaller communities had at least one business parking lot that became a hangout as soon as the business closed. We would hang around unmolested by the local police because "we were just talking, officer." The police did watch us. That is one reason the older people who might have preyed on our groups chose not to hang around. The other is that the group was pretty cohesive when it came to outsiders. Predators pick on strays. In most of those groups there were few who were ever alone. Every decision was modified by the reaction of their peers. Few girls would ever leave a parking lot alone with a boy from out of town let alone an older man.

As a general rule, teens do not socialize much outside their peer group. Social networking sites were originally intended for young professionals, probably single and in their first job. These young people like to go to the latest clubs, see new bands, meet new people and be entertained. The older kids for whom the first social networking sites were originally intended are still going along about their business of networking. Many have moved away from MySpace onto one of the 300+ specialized sites. The ones who are still on MySpace don't care, or even know, that they are being observed by teens. They certainly aren't going to change what they are doing to make sure they do not improperly influence an adolescent. Allowing teens to see and vicariously participate in the world of the post-college Scenester is allowing them to yearn for inappropriate or non-age appropriate things.

Liberally intermixed on SNS are the perverts, porn promoters, mentally twisted and other night creatures each trying to make money or get some sort of thrill from a conversation with a teen if not direct contact. When parents or teachers start trying to keep this from happening the teens have a tendency to react by taking their site private or creating another site with a different name. Taking the site private puts them into an area where they are even more likely to begin an inappropriate conversation. This is important because when you put this book down you are going to try to do something about your child's involvement in SNS. You need to keep an open line of communication and make them understand that you are only trying to keep them safe. If you make it a contest of wills they may just try to become more adept at hiding what they are doing from you.

Daydreaming run amok

Try to envision this: 130 million people, creating different identities within a group, created in an imagined space. Is that not daydreaming run amok? Each teen compares the life he has on these spaces to the one his parents offer and is dissatisfied. Because there is a social aspect to it, each participant sees his world his way. Each world then only intersects like a Venn diagram with the others world. But as a group member, the other members gain the loyalty of the adolescent teen. The teen, who is in that phase of life where he or she is beginning to cleave from their parents, finds it easier to move away. He then accepts the views of the group's members rather than those of his parents. While they may appear shy in their parent's social setting, the children can relate to others on the sites in ways they are afraid to do in person. The life they live on the sites becomes more pleasurable than daily life with their families. But it is primarily built from pixie dust and vivid imagination. **There is plenty of evidence to indicate that they have difficulty telling the difference between life on line and real life.** What is equally frightening to me is that the Kimveer Gill case seems to indicate that the spaces *do* function as a processing point. It allows the users to take the dark imaginings of disturbed minds and develop them first to a belief system and secondly to actions based on those beliefs

". . . numerous studies conducted by leading figures within our medical and public health organizations - our own members - point overwhelmingly to a causal connection between media violence and aggressive behavior in some children. The conclusion of the public health community, based on over 30 years of research, is that viewing entertainment violence can lead to increases in aggressive attitudes, values and behavior, particularly in children.

Joint Statement on the Impact of Entertainment Violence on Children,
Congressional Public Health Summit,
July 26, 2000 American Pediatric Association

Video games and social networking sites are linked. Seldom will you see a male user who does not claim to be a devotee of a video game or online gaming. You don't see a lot of Pokemon either! Most of the sites are geared toward violence and aggression. Video game aggression often bleeds over to social networking sites and takes the form of a verbal or physical assault upon other members of the online community. How many steps are there from video aggression to real aggression? There is significant evidence that certain children, the ones that I describe elsewhere in this text as having wounded spirits, are prime candidates for using this sort of operant conditioning in concert with the social networking sites to hatch ideas that are anti-social. Participating in online video gaming has the effect of promoting changes in "aggressive attitudes, values and behavior, particularly in children." Therefore participating in SNS has the tendency to lead to whatever attitudes, values and behavior that is promoted by those sites.

(Keep in mind – I'm not advocating a global revolt against online gaming – I'm warning you, the parent, about things that might affect your child. WDE)

The Internet: information provider or propaganda ministry

There is a great deal of power in being able to disseminate information. The current view of the Jewish people is at a high point in the West. At the beginning of the 20th century it was at a low. Part of that was because of a single book, ***Der Giftpilz (The Poisonous Mushroom)*** distributed by the Nazi party. The book horribly influenced world thinking about the Jewish nation. Its effect on the German people was almost too horrible to fathom. That single book probably could be faulted for establishing the mindset of German people that led to the death of over 6 million people. Unlike a book, social networking sites are updated regularly. Rather than being an academic reading they are what as known as a personal medium.

Being a personal medium is what helps MySpace and radio be successful at changing minds. Billboards along the highway do not carry the same impact as the radio. A person's radio is almost a part of his private thoughts. A billboard only tells him a small piece of information about the location of food, gasoline or in some cases, serves to promote the image of a national firm. What he hears on the radio is more likely to be incorporated into his personal beliefs almost as if he is listening to himself think. This is true of the social networking site. The user is more likely to internalize beliefs he learns on the internet or myspace because he construes it to be private. But like radio and billboards there are other people behind the scenes that are not that evident.

At the end of the Yellow Brick road, Dorothy, the Tin Man, the Lion and Toto speak to the huge imposing face of the Wizard of Oz. Toto, the dog, pulls aside a green curtain to reveal that the huge image of the Wizard is being manipulated by an old man pulling levers and twisting knobs on the control boards of a fantastic contraption. The Wizard they have been hoping to learn from turns out to be nothing magical at all. It was a manmade device that controlled thinking and behavior in a highly structured society. (The Wizard of Oz, 1939)

The sites open up onto a world stage and serve as a conduit which can be manipulated by the "man behind the green curtain" That man is the mass marketer in this instance. From a position far outside the public view and intent only to sell advertising, he peddles his wares oblivious to what effect the users have on one another. The marketing tools themselves are not the problem, it is the poisonous messages the advertising medium places before the audience. This is what happened to the German people when they did not look at *Der Giftpilz* with the proper amount of healthy skepticism. It was presented in a slick package and it seemed to offer a solution. The result was a society that has been forever burdened as one who accepted a horrible crime against humanity. The episode became part of their national identity.

Most of us cannot conceptualize 130 million users. Therefore the potential for interaction with 130 million other people and their mixed messages is not all that scary. Users think of the site as, well: my space. And we think we share it with only a few friends and don't understand the power it has to mold opinion.

Chapter Six

SOCIAL DISORDER

—ɱ—

Making a name for yourself

True identity comes from accomplishment. How many times have you recounted an advertisement to your friends or co-workers because it made an impression? Perhaps it was particularly funny or had a deep message. Do you remember finishing your description with, "I don't really remember what they were advertising, but the commercial was cool?" You will not really remember the product until you have some experience with it. If that experience is successful you will remember the product. If it removes stains, improves your life or makes a difference, you will remember it. This is why you get free samples at the supermarket.

People are like that. You remember the ones that get things done. If they improve your life or encourage you, you like them. You remember them. They have an identity and character. In the movie, *As Good As It Gets*, Jack Nicholson delivers a line to Helen Hunt that made every woman in the audience gasp. "You make me want to be a better man." Every woman who heard it fantasized that there was something they could do to effect such a change in their man. We don't just want to look better, we want to be better.

Nothing exists in the social networking environment that is either like this or helps to develop this type of behavior in its participants. In fact it seems to feed off of the weaknesses of human nature.

Those weaknesses tend toward the more animalistic behaviors that we are working to change as parents.

Fads come and go.

When you first look at social networking sites they do not appear to be different from any other social phenomenon or fad that has come along in my lifetime. Years ago, there was concern that Rock and Roll was going to destroy our youth. It didn't, but it changed our society greatly. There is a difference between Rock and Roll music and what it came to represent, which was freedom. That freedom led to musicians championing a movement that brought about another cultural change: questioning authority. We worried with good reason about the Aquarian movement (Also known as the Hippie Movement) with it's admonitions to "up the establishment." To the beat of rock music, social reformers encouraged our children to engage in free love and tune in, turn on and drop out. I'll let you be the judge of whether that was a good thing. The use of birth control medication has led to a totally different attitude about sex. This in turn led us to where we are with the plague of pornography.

Did you see her navel?

As a person soon entering my sixth decade, I've been both partic-ipant and observer of many changes in what *is* and *is not* acceptable. Those changes happen slowly and in small increments. Playboy Magazine hit the stands in 1953 with the philosophy that it would show "tasteful" partially nude women and promote a somewhat hedonistic lifestyle bound in fine wine, high-brow parties and good clean sex. This was a fundamental shift in thinking for the time. In the early fifties, the nuclear, two parent family was the ideal. Divorce was considered a failure of character and conscience. Morality was understood widely if not defined closely by the courts. There were no mainstream magazines for men that catered to a lifestyle of romancing women without the implied intent of getting married and producing a family. The publisher of that magazine started slowly, showing pretty girls, nice clothing, good wines and liquors. It was an attempt to define a group identity for men who wanted a high-flying life style; men who did not want families.

What few will remember is that the first nudes were on a par with today's commercial for Victoria's Secret or Oil of Olay. At that time, the women photographed for those magazines seldom, if ever exposed their navel. Sometimes only the breasts and parts of the buttocks were exposed. The publisher started out slowly, not intending to tweak the noses of the establishment too badly. I remember that it made local news when the first issue appeared in which the model's navel was exposed. In light of today's fashions it seems ironic to me that a teenaged girl will hardly go anywhere unless she is dressed in a way that exposes her tummy. Later a similar fuss was made the first time Playboy began to feature models whose **pubic area** was shown. I hope this does not portend the next fashion trend in teen fashion.

At this point, our culture is ripe for another shift that I believe will be greatly influenced by social networking. The point is this: Big changes in culture begin with small steps. My opinion is that social networking sites amount to a bit more than just a step. I believe it is dangerous to think of social networking as *only* a fad.

Image – Looking Good

In our 21st century culture we tend to think that if something looks good, it must be good. There is much talk about our image. Image is nothing without the substance of character. It is dangerous to try to look the part when there is no substance to back it up. Men without ability who press themselves into the middle of stressful situations usually fail.

During the Vietnam War we became aware of fragging, that is, shooting or hand-grenading the officer who sends you out into the field. Perhaps as many as 600 officers were murdered, and another 1400 died mysteriously. The stories that came home from that war about fragging were usually about leaders who failed to lead in combat. In that conflict, good military officers had no problem getting their people to fight. They led by example and took care of their soldiers, never asking them to do the impossible or to risk their lives. One should not get used to the idea that he can get by on looks alone.

Reinforcing good looks

When one spends a good deal of time on the social networking sites, he gets the idea that looking good is very important. One has to have many friends to feel good regardless how real those friends are. If one is to be appreciated, one must wear the right clothes and acquire the right look. Therefore if you look good, you have accomplished something and you must be a good person. The cool people have an entourage. If not that, they belong to an entourage or at least a gaggle of similarly attired friends. They are cool because they look cool. Just because your site has cool graphics and you like all of the same nationally advertised merchandise that everyone else likes, you must be cool. Of course all the girls must have short tops and low slung pants that expose their tummies. The boys wear shirts that emphasize the torso and every chance they get they have their shirts off. The more skin you show, the more people ask to be your friend on your SNS. If people are constantly asking to be added to your site *you must be cool*. That is a false assumption and the benefits are questionable at best.

Present oriented.

Looking good is part of what is called a "present oriented" culture. A person who lives only for the moment values time differently. One example of persons who live only for the moment is in a class of people society calls: criminals. They are highly impulsive and prone to do only that which feels good right now. Like an adolescent, these folks do not really appreciate the benefits of delayed gratification. I have often argued that most people become criminals because of adolescent thinking. There is not a lot of difference in the mindset of the criminal and the adolescent.

A study was done in 1959 of two groups of incarcerated male and female subjects. Results showed them to be very present minded as compared to the general population. The same study was done again in 1974. In each case the testing involved a gift of money and how the inmates would spend or distribute it. In 1959 the inmates mentioned giving the money to others inside and outside the jail. There was so little drug use during the late 50's that drugs were not even mentioned. By 1974 no inmate mentioned giving the money to others but they frequently mentioned keeping it to buy drugs. (Siberman, 1978) The current MTV generation is even more impulsive and prefers immediate rather than delayed gratification. The MTV folks even keep the commercials moving and jumping so that there is little chance for your child's mind to wander. The music videos jump from scene to scene, the musicians move, change clothing from scene to scene and are constantly changing. Doing so is a conscious decision by the people who produce those shows. They know that the constant movement keeps the attention focused on the action and that the child is less likely to get up and do something else during commercial. So the commercials look just like the show. Adolescents love this sort of thing because the "brain noise" that a kid has at this time keeps them from hearing almost everything anyone says to them. Their brains are floating in a chemical soup full of hormones that influences everything they do. They are learning fast and everything is new and exciting. They like it that way. Every time the pace slows down they get anxious.

Defending a boring life

In a private conversation with Michael Karpovich, one of America's best motivational speakers (info@speakerresource. com), made a very important point. Mr. Karpovich said we tend to think that everyone except us is leading some sort of fantastic life. He polled the room in a recent seminar. In a room of two hundred people only two had been to a party over the last weekend. None had been to a nightclub recently, danced the night away, shared drinks with runway models or taken a jet to a romantic island for dinner. Most of us had just gone home, tended to our pets, washed clothes and loved our families. Social networking tells your child that such a life is boring. In fact one of the most frequently heard words in your house if you have children is probably going to be this word, *boring*. Children who do not have a very intact set of rules for behavior and conduct are quickly influenced. On social networking they will learn that life should never be boring and that partying with your friends is an end unto itself. This is not a very new idea. It is a variation on the Flower Power generation (1965-75 roughly) idea of how life should be lived: If it feels good, do it! This is a very empty existence. After the thrill of constant partying begins to wear thin, the party crowd begins to look for other ways to spice up their life. They tend to try to spice their lives with material things. The people on social networking sites promote alcohol, drugs, sexual behaviors and being a part of some idealized scene as real life. It's the users and peers who are teaching this message. The people who have made the sites available are simply trying to sell merchandise. While I may not see eye-to-eye with them on their ethics, nothing they are doing is illegal. They are not necessarily promoting this behavior merely by making the sites available. Some of the users of the sites are very conscientious as well – but – a lot of the users are promoting some very poor choices. Teens and young adults who are looking for answers will be deluded into believing that these things represent solutions.

Persistently Vegetative Adolescence

Within the last forty to fifty years, that period following WWII, a certain portion of our population has followed a divergent path toward maturity. We have a population now, the members of which have grown up without a universally agreed upon creed or set of beliefs. Instead our children are being taught a sort of relativism that eliminates absolutes and focuses the individual on himself. The result has been a culture in which a large number of people have a profound lack of maturity. If that sounds like a big leap let me explain. It is a path or a state of being that I will christen: Persistently Vegetative Adolescence.

> **Persistent**: constantly repeated; continued: *persistent noise.*
> **Vegetative**: characterized by a lack of activity; inactive; passive: *a vegetative state.*
> **Adolescence**: a period or stage of development, as of a society, preceding maturity.

In other words our people are not growing up. They are the product of an earlier generation that said we should question authority and "put down the establishment." In fact, the leaders of the movements of the late 60's and 70's came close to anarchy in their teaching. The children of those people are the "thirty-somethings" that are now pushing the current interest in being a part of the "scene."

Modern day PVAs have repackaged the components of Marxism/Communism as part of a set of progressive or intellectual beliefs that have taken on all the attributes of a religion if not a charismatic cult. Part of that set of beliefs is teaching children a way of thinking that focuses upon feeling rather than logic or truth. Children who are taught to feel are easier to manipulate politically than children who are taught to think. Feeling children only react to stimuli. Thinking children will only react after making a critical analysis based on whatever creed or code of conduct they have been taught.

In the post-war period, we began a cultural shift as the parents of the baby boomers tried to give us a better life. For whatever reason, either because of guilt or misplaced desire to create our own utopia, we produced a significant number of children who did not internalize the norms of our larger society. We, as a culture, gave up all of the time tested methodologies for raising children. Dr. Spock and Dr. This and Dr. That gave us every excuse for not doing things the way our "establishment" parents taught us. Instead, we became permissive and "conscious" of our children's developmental needs. Parents became buddies rather than fathers and mothers. Each participant began a headlong race to become the best "me" that they could possibly become.

The PVAs of this generation presumed to throw progressively noisy and dangerous protest demonstrations that were without rational basis. Each can be equated to a "temper tantrum" of a pre-adolescent child. These were not the peaceful protests of Dr. Martin Luther King. They were methodological replications of those protests for sure, but they lacked the lofty purpose. King was dealing with true cultural and social injustice and asked only that the black race be granted the same rights guaranteed every American. Those who followed protested US involvement in the Vietnam War, environmental issues, and other popular causes. Although their causes may have had legitimate ends, over time their methodology degenerated to less noble devices. They no longer wanted justice according to the rules, they wanted to change the rules altogether. Eventually some of the more radical of them decided they wanted their way even if it broke the rules. Wanting to change the rules or rebelling against them is a prime characteristic of adolescence. Those arrested adolescents of permissive parents didn't like the rules grown-ups used to live their lives and we have let them get away with it.

Each of these "politically active" youth became parents, ran for political office and began to vote for like minded candidates who made their way into government with the basic plan to "change things." One of the common themes in political discourse in all parties Democrat, Independent, Republican, is "vote for change." Many candidates are guilty of asking us to "change" things without telling us what those changes would be. The more vague they are about change, the more likely the voter is to believe they are planning to change things their way. This is called *Magical Thinking*, something we discussed earlier that is also usually found in adolescents.

Politically, we often ask ourselves "are the inmates running the asylum?" The truth is, **adolescents are in charge** they just happen to be well past adolescence physically and chronologically. If they don't like the results of a presidential election: "You cheated!" If the PVAs don't like who is going to choose our next round of judges: "We'll hold our breath till we turn blue in the face." Of course they call it a filibuster, but it's only a matter of semantics. In Texas when state legislators didn't get their way, they "ran away from home."[14] Those legislators may be over 21, but in practical application they are children nonetheless. When parents take the shortcut of bullying children through constant criticism they are acting like adolescents. When young parents succumb to drugs and alcohol and leave raising their children to their grandparents; they are acting like adolescents. When men ignore raising their children and the Attorney General of the State has to track them down to get child support; they are acting like adolescents. Even the young professional, who gets fussy with the waiter and sends his steak back a couple of times at a fancy restaurant — is behaving like an adolescent. I would say that grown men who attend sports events, paint their chests and hoot for . . . but that's football, which is clinically an obsession. So I'll skip that one.

As a result of the large number of PVAs in the general population, the United States is full of young people who have suffered from parents who never learned to parent. They are stuck in a mindset that originated in a time of social change that focused on feeling good, expressing one's self sexually; with having multiple partners; and having little personal responsibility. Our society stood by wringing our hands as they fundamentally changed our society. They tried to shift focus onto children's supposed natural goodness. They wanted us to learn from their example. Their methods have been tried and have failed. I hope we will soon come to understand that our culture is suffering from a profound lack of maturity.

Children do not naturally have character, love of country, and a belief that one works for the common good. Any parent knows that if you let a two year old get away with it, he or she will become a tyrant in your home. The PVA parents failed their children by focusing on feelings rather than a creed or set of standards. One is properly trained to be a parent, by being properly parented. These kids have grown up with little or no sense of responsibility. They come from good homes, broken homes, homes of single parents, absent parents, rich people and people of poverty and neglect. They are a generation of children raised by immature adults who have no understanding of maturity or how to achieve it. These parentless children continue to produce children who do not know how to be parents. At this point we have about two or three generations that represent a subculture within our culture. Many of these children suffer from what is sometimes called "wounded spirits." (Dobson, 2001) Unconsciously, these children attempt very early in life to recreate their own perfect family unit. The result is teen pregnancy, early marriage and a repetition of the cycle. Complicating the issue is the almost sure failure of these children to be successful at a relationship. Having failed at their attempt to become what they most desire, compounds the hopelessness and anger they feel from being abandoned or poorly treated by their parents. Had I not come to understand how being failed or abused by parents affected children, I might not have understood the dangers they face in this society. I also would not have understood how difficult it is to be a child today. I would have failed to recognize the dangers that online social networking websites present. At your local school, there are children of all types. Some children have been blessed with positive parenting. In the normal school setting these children actually help each other cope with life by example even when they don't intend to. They learn from each other in class, in the halls and in the recreation areas. They all know that being a teenager is a tough business. They form groups and dyads that allow them to get through four years of high school.

In *Lord of the Flies* an allegorical novel by Nobel Prize-winning author William Golding a group of young boys are stranded on a desert island and must negotiate the social problems of cooperation and self-government. The theme is an attempt to trace the defects of society back to the defects of human nature. In the story the boys try to structure their society on the rules they were taught at home. Over time, and without the reinforcement of their elders, their society begins a slide into jungle rule and animalistic behaviors. Any time teens get together there is a *Lord of the Flies* quality to their behavior. Any public school teacher or youth leader can tell you it is true. That quality is carried over into their online conversations.

SNS has the potential to be a platform for continuing this persistently vegetative state where image trumps substance. It will continue to allow the pooling of ignorance that will perpetuate animalistic behavior. How many more generations will fail to mature and only learn responsibility after experiencing loss or suffering emotional harm?

Finally, <u>if social networking is not specifically designed to take advantage of the weakest and most vulnerable part of adolescence, it is hard to imagine what a more specifically designed program would look like.</u> If your child is an emotionally driven child or is especially quick to get his or her feelings hurt, a myspace is probably something you should monitor really well. Most likely, it will perpetuate <u>the creation of more kids who do not understand maturity</u>. I am sure that the majority of our children can romp around on SNS and never be affected. They can converse with their friends and move on to something else. But, that does not lessen the effect it can have on the minority. You know your child. Which route will they take?

Chapter Seven

HOW DO WE FIX THIS MESS?

—⚯—

Who has oversight?

Right now, you are probably reading this thinking: "Someone needs to be told!" "There must be some governmental agency!" "Don't we have boards and commissions that have oversight of this sort of thing?" The answer for the moment is that there is _no effective oversight_. Moreover, the sites are designed in such a way to eliminate oversight; and, there is good evidence to suggest that some of the sites owners do not want oversight. They fear that it will suppress interest in the sites. You might ask why are they so concerned about someone suppressing interest in a site that they are giving away free? Since you are an adult you know there is nothing free, let's start with that.

It's in the numbers

What makes these sites dangerous is the same thing that makes them successful. It is the large number of people who participate. The most widely known site has well over 130 million subscribers. That is your child and 129, 999,999 other impressionable kids. Keep that figure in mind. Keep in mind too that word impressionable.

Now let's discuss advertising. If you want to place an advertisement in a magazine or newspaper you pay by the column inch. The per inch cost is calculated using a formula that takes into account the number of times it will show up in the paper, how much space it takes, the number of people who take the paper in your community and so forth. If the paper has hundreds of subscribers the price is less than if the paper has thousands of subscribers. A garage sale add in Podunk is around $10 while in a larger community it might be $24.99. So, if more people see your advertisement, you pay more to advertise.

One of the ways of measuring advertising's effectiveness is *impressions*. Every time someone sees a logo or picture of your product he forms an idea about the product. This is one impression. I'll bet you thought that was some sort of psycho-social term! It's not, it's an advertising term. Every impression helps to establish firmly what is good, bad, cool, not cool, stylish or nerdy. An advertising medium that has lots of subscribers and therefore makes lots of impressions can demand high rates for that advertising space.

Social network advertising

Now let's look at advertising on the social networking sites. Every time a user moves from page to page in the site, small windows open around him making advertising impressions. If advertising is not popping up in windows, it is blinking in the borders. An instant message window takes up about 20% of the screen. The rest of the screen constantly changes. Impressions are being made literally out of the corner of your child's eye. Every time a new advertising impression pops up, 130 million young brains form some sort of opinion about the product. You can see from the math that this number of impressions should be expensive. My best information tells me that a single day for one advertisement on MySpace is twenty to forty thousand dollars. There are hundreds of them every day on the major sites. The owners are getting rich "giving away" the free site to your child. Why? It works! The users see and admire the products and go buy them. Therefore, the persons who sell advertising space have no reason to suppress the number of people using the sites by policing who gets on them. The more, the better!

Some might say that critics of social networking sites are just jealous of the money being made by these sites. But that is not the point at all. There is nothing wrong with advertising per se. Advertising informs us about new products that may be beneficial.

That's a good thing. The point is that these sites – even Vampire Freaks.Com – have a profit motive. They are selling stuff! People with a profit motive are eager to make buying impressions on your child **regardless the propriety, moral content or whether your child is of the age to deal with it appropriately.** While that may not be true in every case, it is true often enough to make you pay more attention.

Who is going to help the confused kids and their parents?

One of my goals for this book it to make the behavioral health and counseling communities think about this issue. Enough clinical people read the first drafts of this book for me to be assured that most professionals are going to see the point I have made. Understanding parent/child interactions and helping parents deal with the effects of long term use of the internet has already begun. In the Journal of Professional Counseling (Fall 2005) there is an article about Internet addiction.

> The rapid development and increased availability of the Internet has led some researchers to examine the effects excessive usage has on an individual's social, emotional, cognitive and physical development. Pathological Internet use has become more common is society. To address this concern, Internet addiction has been added to the mental health lexicon. (Watson, 2005)

The author goes on to say that research has led to the development of standards for diagnosing and assessing clients who suffer from this addiction. Research is necessary by people more educated than I in the area of identity manipulation or identity changes as a result of SNS. I have an idea of how the research should be done, but making the results statistically valid will require a professional long term study.

Internet addiction has been shown to have affects on the social, psychological and occupational areas of life. It has the quality of many addictions, more use: less of a "kick." The users then increase their use in search of the same response. Internet Addition and SNS identity changes are similar in that they have effects that the user did not originally intend when he started to use the computer. Those in the counseling field would benefit from some methodologies that will help in treating those patients dealing with SNS. Perhaps that will be my next book.

Let the government do it!

The government is going to be slow about recognizing the danger of social networking. They will be even slower drafting and passing legislation. There will be cries of censorship, anti-business, freedom of expression, and so on. Even if they started today, your newborn might be able to vote before a substantial change is accomplished. ***Therefore, the only way you have of seeing to it that your child's life is not changed by these sites is to do it yourself.***

There is no fix for this mess!

Update: During the period when I was writing this book, Senator Mark Foley resigned from Congress because of inappropriate email he sent to pages serving the legislature. One of the pages told the press the whole thing is based on a series of hoax instant messages that were sent by pages for a joke. Depending upon how this plays out – our government could get a little more interested in studying the issue of internet use and create some new law.

Chapter Eight

WILL LEGAL INTERVENTIONS HELP?

—ɯɯ—

Real intervention is needed

This is an era, when computers can have a conversation with a teen and he will not even know that it is a computer. We have algorithms embedded in email, voice mails, and telephone listening devices that can pick out key phrases of a terrorist in conversation with his Mullah back in Iraq or Afghanistan – and notify the National Security Agency. Social networking sites need a similar device to pick out the scary language. The program could identify the Kimveer Gills and *point them out to someone*. It would not take too much to form an alliance with some agency, local or national. The same could be done with say the National Suicide Hotline when there were too many uses of terms related to pre-suicidal behavior. If we can keep track of what jeans a kid wears we should be able to keep track of how many times he has promoted violence or ranted about killing his fellow man.

New legislation is needed that will protect privacy rights but recognize that the *internet is a public place.* Just as there are rules for behavior on a city street, there should be similar laws governing behavior on SNS that place only a slim barrier to admission. The barrier to admission into these places serves the supplier with potential economic benefit and really offers no assurance of safety that one would get from a more exclusive membership – your health club or country club for instance. Internet bullying should be a crime. Excessively violent speech should be a crime and probable cause to investigate the criminal intent and/or mental stability of the speaker.

Any kid under 18 should have to provide the email address and credit card number of an adult. The adult would then set the parameters for conversation and site content of the user. When that user went to a site on a pre-selected list of addresses, an email could automatically be generated to the adult's email address. The reason for the credit card is that the adult should have an incentive to watch the underage child's surfing. Each notification should cost the adult a few bucks. This should be mandatory if the child has done anything of a violent nature in the juvenile justice system. It should be a part of his probation that any computer he used, if he used one at all, would notify his probation officer. We already restrict the use of computers by people who commit crimes with them. To expand that restriction is not unreasonable.

The security sections of the spaces have taken some steps to keep the perverts and other riff raff off the sites. They say that they are trying to make it more difficult for young and old to reach each other in ways that harm the younger persons. But there is nothing to keep your 15 year old daughter from willingly or unintentionally participating in a relationship either on line or in reality with an older man. There is nothing to prevent your teenaged son from beginning a relationship with an older woman if they want to keep it from you. Given the number of recent instances of teachers having sex with their students, what are the odds that something like this is happening between older and younger users of social networking?

In 2004, teacher Debra LaFave had sex with a fourteen year old from her reading class. She plead guilty after first blaming the incident on being bi-polar. Pamela Rogers Turner, a teacher in Florida, had sex with her 13 year old student. She sent him sexually inappropriate nude photographs over the internet. She pleaded guilty. When she got out of jail she violated the terms of her parole by blogging about the experience and talking about having sex with him. Mary Kay LeTourneau shocked the nation in the 90's by having a long term relationship with a 13 year old boy who she later married.

This is important!

It should be apparent at this point that these sites have a strong probability of negatively influencing your child. As I have said repeatedly, what kids learn on these sites is peer driven and therefore one of the hardest types of knowledge for a parent to combat. Secondly, the *chance* that social networking sites are going to have safeguards placed on their operations is slim.

Nine

ANTIPATHY FOR CHRISTIANS AND GOODNESS

—⁓—

Shut up the Jesus Freaks

One of the things most often attacked on these sites is religion and Christianity. That is not to say that some of the bulletins and messages are not sent by good kids to other good kids about Christianity. One of the first assaults you will find by studying the personal spaces is the admonition "Tell all the Jesus Freaks to shut the h— up!" My personal belief is that these sites are here to stay for the near future. I would challenge every Christian community to find a way to use IM and social networking to bring more children into contact with God's word. The opportunity for someone to influence society greatly exists with the advent of social networking. Christian's world wide should look carefully and plan how they will use websites to reach out on a personal basis. The opposition has a head start. Recently Facebook has added a religion field to their site. This happened just before this book went to press. Their note regarding the addition said that it was in response to user requests. Xanga is a community that supports weblogs and blogging. There are a lot of religious discussions posted by Zangans. This is good and offers a starting place for knowledgeable Christians. .

Discussions about religion of any sort are often discouraged. Not necessarily by the owners of the sites but by the users. You don't usually find religious topics unless you go looking for them. Because of the list of friends my son started with, he had a large group of Christian friends to begin with – and the list grew. That is not typical.

There is something fundamental that I want to discuss about Christianity, this culture and how that too is connected to my concerns about social networking. This country was founded on Christian values. This is not really arguable. You can read a lot of revisionist history that tries to lessen the impact Christianity had on the creation and development of this country, but the majority of it is bunk. The truth of the matter is that we would not be all that different from other countries if we were not Christian. Because I believe in Christ, I believe our nation has been blessed. It is blessed because this nation has used Christian principles in its formation and in the development of the Constitution and Bill of Rights. We formed the union to allow our people to be free from having to worship under a state religion as our forefathers did in England. Because we have grown up in a Christian nation, most of us take for granted that Christian values are American values. They are, but they were Christian first. Many people only want to recognize them as American and think that they can tweak them a little bit to make them better by making us more like other countries. You need to understand the importance of the source for those values. It's not OK for them to be American, but not Christian. Let's get right to the salient point: If these values were not Christian, you would not be able to criticize them. Free will is a Christian value. Freedom of thought is a value that Christ taught his disciples. Self ownership rather than being owned by the State is a Christian teaching. Democracy is a Christian value placing power with the people. Having personal worth independent of your boss or your government is a Christian value. Everything that happens in this country, in our government and on the social networking site, can happen only because this country was created by Christians to allow freedom for the common man. Few other countries allow that kind of freedom. Christian teachings are positive, they do not seek to tear down others or be critical. Social networking encourages ridicule. Christians seek a life that has substance. Social networking promotes image.

You want your child to have character

Christians want their children to first accept the word of God and Christ. From that acceptance a child begins to build what we call character. One can argue that the traits that make up good character can be taught without teaching about Christ. But it is to ignore the fact that those values are ones taught by Christ. You train your child through years of grade school, Sunday school, club activities and fraternal organizations. Later in life, he or she may get very involved in study that explains the deep theological issues that compose the grace of God. But those matters are something that a neophyte does not understand early. Grace is accepted through faith. There is no place on earth more likely to attack that faith than a social networking site. This is ironic to me since their first attack on God is that you can't see him. It's ironic because they are speaking from a place that is primarily an imagined space!

My son was a regular in church and a professing Christian. He had completed all of the steps to become an Eagle Scout except for the final project. He had been a wonderful child and a willing learner in grade school and Junior High. Despite that training, he learned to pepper his conversations with a lot of four letter words he learned from his social networking pals. He got the courage he needed from talking with his friends about their parents – remember a high percentage of them hate their parents – to tell us off in a blast of expletives. He lost respect for the three people on this earth that had for many years supported everything he had attempted to accomplish. He chose to pick a fight with his mother and me because we would not allow him to wear the *right* clothes or to wear them the way the kids on the scene wear them. He learned that his parents were out of step with all of the social networking values and chose to fight us over them. The idea that parents are out of step is perpetuated in television shows that portray parents as stupid and unnecessarily rigid. A character in a crime drama recently told the detectives looking for her friend that she was not to blame for the way her life turned out. Her parents wouldn't let her "hang out" or "have a boyfriend" when she was "already fifteen years old."

Our culture does not support character building

The children of baby boomers now populate our schools and the state agencies that determine the needs of our educational system. These folks have removed teaching of Christianity and yet they don't know how to deal with issues like kids being bullies. They want to teach conservation but they ignore what the oldest book on the subject says about protecting the earth. They want to help the poor but they don't look to the methods for providing for the poor that date back five millennia. They want to know the future, but they ignore the one book that has prophesied correctly the events of the future for that same five thousand year period. No other collection of writings, Nostradamas included, has that kind of record.

Social networking is focused on everything but character building, a relationship with Christ and connection to a religion. Their answer about the basic questions most children have about life is a message that says consumerism provides happiness. Social networking is just not a good place for your adolescent to spend a lot of time – especially unsupervised time. During adolescence they should be spending as much time with their parents as they spend with peers. That's the only way you are going to unwind them from the doofus notions their peers give them. Who is going to explain right and wrong to them, you or that pimply faced kid in geometry class? Who is going to tell them if God is real or the purpose of life and death? Are you going to leave that to xxxomfgImsohot at a MySpace site in Dubuque, Iowa?

I am not the only professional who looks to the Bible for sources of strength and for instruction. Psychologist and personality, James Dobson, who wrote what as far as I am concerned, are *the* books about raising boys and discipline, points to this scripture, and I agree:

> "And these word, which I command thee this day, shall be in thine heart: and thou shalt teach them diligently unto they children, and shalt talk of them when thou sittest in thine house, and when thou walketh by the way, and when thou liest down, and when thou risest up. And thou shalt bind them for a sign upon thine hand, and they shall be as front-

lets between thine eyes. And thou shalt write them upon the posts of thy house, and on thy gates.

Deuteronomy 6:6-9 OKJV

If you are to develop your child's spirituality you must teach them that there is right and wrong. Teach them that God's will is the ultimate for the determination of right and wrong – you will die a happy parent. If you do not feel particularly spiritual, take your child to church and get active. You only have to be one step ahead to lead. You child will squirm and protest at first but they will secretly enjoy the attention and the opportunity to learn at your side. You will learn too!

THE SAGA OF RICK ROKR

—ɯɯ—

The Saga Begins

R ick Rokr is one of the pseudonyms that my son chose for himself on his MySpace accounts. Rick was a pretty cool guy. The boy who would become Rick Rokr was born into a lower class family in a suburb of Phoenix. His parents named him Ricky. They were a beer drinking, party couple, with four children. Mom could only do a limited amount of work. She eventually found that she could sell or participate in the sale of drugs to supplement that income. Conveniently, it also provided a solution to the daily boredom of tending to four youngsters while her husband was away on construction sites. She eventually showed him how he could chase away his demons with a drug called – methamphetamine.

By the time Ricky was four, the other children had already been in State Custody twice. At that point the law caught up simultaneously with both parents and they were given jail sentences. The children were placed with their uncle who already had three children. At some time during that stay, their maternal Grandfather showed up and volunteered to take them away for the weekend. The uncle was more than happy to oblige. The grandfather disappeared and Child Protective Services, local law enforcement and, if they were telling the truth, the family, did not know how to find the children. Some time later authorities came to believe that the grandfather was an alcoholic pedophile.

Ricky and his siblings spent eleven months riding around with their maternal grandfather in his car. The grandfather was supposedly working his way to Austin, Texas. Sometime during the journey the children were told the house was sold. I suspect it was sold for back taxes. The move may have been a ruse simply to get the children out of Phoenix.

The grandfather worked as a day laborer. At quitting time he would drink beer with his coworkers and then come back to where ever he had left the children. He was often drunk. He was frequently too forgetful, or too broke to buy food for the children. My daughter has told me of times when they would get Cheerio's and save them to eat one at a time so they would always have a little something. They frequently scrounged in the neighborhood around wherever they were living for things to eat. During those times my daughter began to believe that they were going to starve to death. She is prone to tears when discussing that period of her life.

Life on the Road with Grandfather

They stayed on the road living out of the car and various motel rooms until police found them. Police were responding to a suspicious person call at a Central Texas motel room after the maids reported to the manager they had seen the man fondling one of the girls. The four children aged, 4, 8, 9 &10 were found with a disheveled man in his fifties; their grandfather. They were taken into protective custody, dirty, hungry and scared. For some reason the officer chose to put the children in her car and have their grandfather follow her to the police station. He went to his car and was never seen again. Several years later, I found that he had died from complications of severe alcohol abuse.

It was never conclusively confirmed that any of the children were assaulted sexually. Therefore there was not enough evidence to make a case in court. The four children remained in State Custody for the next four years. Only one of them ever really had a successful relationship with an adult. During their childhood adults repeatedly failed them. This hit Ricky particularly hard.

Early wounds

When Ricky and his sister came to live with us they were both rail thin even though they had been living in foster care for over four years. We quickly learned they did not want to get accustomed to eating a lot just in case lean times returned. Because of the neglect they never got used to sweets and Ricky never particularly wanted candy or sweets until several years later after he developed a relationship with sweet eating peers. A half gallon of ice cream would stay in our freezer for months. They never ate all of their Halloween candy and often the remainder would spoil. Even though we have consistently told my daughter that anything in the refrigerator is hers for the taking, she always asks for permission to get food. The impact on their lives from this experience cannot be measured.

Foster Care

After they were found by police Ricky and his siblings were taken into protective custody by the Texas Department of Family and Protective Services. They were placed in a foster home in Central Texas. The foster mother was a Hispanic lady with little education and a part time job working as a maid in a hotel. Her husband had an hourly job with a local government agency as a mechanic. The garage of the home was his only place of refuge. He was always working on cars in his garage but I saw him as a man with very little ambition. He had very little input into how the house was managed. She was a frustrated person who might be described as an overly ambitious underachiever. She aspired to be upwardly mobile and a member of the middle class. Her only claim to that status was her spic and span house. He stayed out of it in order to keep peace

She took in the children and gave them two rooms. Two girls stayed in one room and two boys in the other. For this service she got approximately $1600 to $2000 every month in what the state likes to call "reimbursement" for helping to raise the children. Had she spent the money on their care it would have been fine. Instead she shopped for them at Goodwill and spent a good deal of the money accessorizing her home. The foster mother required them to stay in their rooms during most of the day. They were given a television and a gaming machine. From later discussions of those games with my son I realize that from 5 to 9 of age years he was spending a good deal of his time playing games that were meant for teens and mature audiences. The foster mother was neither intelligent enough to understand the damage these games could do nor did she care enough to become involved. During these early years, Ricky learned to lose himself inside the environs of a fantasy world by playing games for hours.

As the oldest boy became a teen he became somewhat rebellious. The foster mom was prone to loudly berate them for any thing she thought was inappropriate. She was in mid-rant over an incident with a bicycle, when he pushed her. She fell against some Venetian blinds and broke a window. She demanded CPS remove him from the home. That was ten years ago and he is no longer a child. We still get to visit him occasionally. After all this time he still remembers the incident and wishes he could have held his temper.

The women in his life

The oldest sister had always positioned herself as the protector of this little family unit. She had previously protected them from their Grandfather when they were on the road. I suspect she did so at her own expense, mentally and physically. She was very unhappy that one of them had been separated from the group. It was only a matter of months before brooding righteous indignation over this incident caused her to attack the foster parent. Ricky then lost the sister that had been the little sibling group's protector when the foster mom demanded she be removed. She was somewhat of a mother figure by this time

Ricky lost his biological mother because she could not control her appetite for drugs and alcohol; he lost his sister because she could not control her temper. Ricky was daily criticized by his foster parent and told he was too much trouble. (*How I wish I could have spent those years with him. WDE*) The foster mom did not like to deal with active children and was constantly being very hateful and mean. She would not let the kids play like normal kids do and could not tolerate their making a mess.

They were sequestered in their rooms even when the foster mom's family came to visit. The family would often have a barbeque in the back yard but the kids could not join in the fun. The children were not allowed to be a part of the meals or celebrations and had to stay in their rooms. One July 4th the family shot off fireworks after the barbeque. Ricky and his sister would recount with conspiratorial glee the fact that they had sneaked into the dining room and watched the fireworks through the window.

By this time Ricky had pretty much lost respect for women. It is normal for boys and girls in foster care to blame the foster mom for everything that happens that they don't like. Every parent knows that children go through periods where they really don't like one or the other of his or her parents. This happens when the parent gets too involved in playing the role of disciplinarian without having a strong relationship built or when the parent does not model good behaviors. Ricky's foster mom played the role of a strident harpy who could not be pleased.

My wife was their therapist

We became acquainted with the children because my wife was their therapist for over three years. She provided therapy sessions in the foster home while they were in care. Of course she knew and saw the boys too. Therefore she witnessed a good deal of what happened. It was part of the reason we chose to adopt them. Ricky and his sister became very dependent upon each other while they were in foster care. While his sister was cute and shy he was rambunctious and outgoing. My wife and I were aghast when we learned the foster parent had talked a doctor into prescribing drugs because of Ricky's behavior. Somehow the foster mom convinced the doctor that he suffered from ADHD and was highly aggressive. The only excuse she gave my wife was that he would not sit at the dinner table without swinging his feet under the table. The drugs were not appropriate for a child his age.

We adopt

Ricky and his sister were the only children living in the Central Texas foster home after the two older children had been taken away. The original plan had been for the younger daughter of the foster mom and her husband to adopt the two boys. When Ricky's brother "attacked" the foster mom, the couple decided that the boys were not acceptable. By that point my wife was seriously considering trying to adopt his sister. She was still a therapy patient at that point. My wife shyly suggested that of all the children she had seen in several years of practice, this child was the only one she would consider adopting. She hung in the air a rhetorical question: "I just don't know how we would handle having a child?" I think she was surprised when I responded: "The same way we would handle it if your birth control had failed, with God's help." For reasons of conflict of interest she quietly stopped seeing Ricky's sister as a therapist and we began the process of becoming adoptive parents.

Ricky and his sister were adopted into our home in 1999. For months afterwards they could not say a simple declarative sentence without adding the disclaimer: "Just kidding!" They had been brow beaten, criticized and told that they would never amount to anything. They were so traumatized that they could not make the simplest wish known without adding, "Just kidding!" "Could we have pancakes this morning instead of cereal? Just kidding!" "Oh, Spiderman's on at the theater, can we go see it?" "Just kidding"

What did that mean? It meant: "I would like to have something different for breakfast but I've been verbally assaulted in the past for making my wishes known – I don't want it bad enough to argue with you like I did with my foster mom." It took months for us to build enough trust to overcome the habit.

Rick and his sisters.

After we adopted them they were almost like one person. Any suggestion that we made had to be mutually agreeable to both of them. It took several years before they began to operate individually. One of my happiest memories is sitting in my living room listening to them play. Their laughter was infectious and came from the best place in the soul. Ricky was allowed to be off of drugs and be just another rambunctious kid at our house. He had no problems in school, enjoyed his friends, played basketball and attended church camps and Bible Schools. He had a smile that would soften hearts and brighten the room.

This might be a good point to digress and tell you that after the older sister left to live in another home she became aggressive. She lived in a couple of group homes and following her removal we visited her often as possible. They allowed the children to talk alone.

This was a mistake. We became aware very quickly that she was promoting the idea that they should remember "their family" and never sell out to the adoptive parents. She promoted the idea that they remember that we were not their "real parents." In the foster parent world it is known as promoting "failure to attach." When children do not attach to their new families they do not have the investment in that family that would make them willing to follow its rules or accept its values. While this did not affect the younger sister it did confuse Ricky to the point that he found it difficult to fit into our family

It's OK the kids are asleep

During the early years Ricky would argue that he and his sister were going to live together for the rest of their lives. Neither of them wanted to be married and they would buy a house together and that-would-be-that! Of course he was only nine at the time and things changed. During pre-adolescence and right up to the week before he died, Ricky was visibly squeamish about sexual displays, love scenes and mentions of sexual matters. From our evening conversations, I could tell that Ricky felt a lot of pressure from girls for physical contact. My assessment was that he had seen a lot more "real" adult sexual activity than he ever told us about. He had probably seen the first acts of sex acted out by drunken adults. Perhaps this occurred during his earliest years or during his time on the road with his grandfather. From my work in law enforcement and with damaged children, I know that it is not uncommon for people who are using drugs to have sex in the same room with their "sleeping" children. It is probable that Ricky had that kind of experience even if he or his siblings were never molested. On a couple of occasions when he was still with his mother she kicked his father out of the house. In his absence she took a lover who was probably her drug dealer. The opportunity existed that the drug induced behavior caused normal inhibitions to melt away. What he saw we will probably never know. That experience left him highly apprehensive about his own participation in sexual activity. He had difficulty, I believe, in reconciling the ugliness of what he had seen and the longing for physical contact he desired. He did not want to rush into what he knew to be risky behavior. He wanted a safe way to start a relationship. He found it by falling in love with a girl who lived 200 miles away.

During our late night, father/son discussions a new subject was creeping into Ricky's life. He began to talk about girls. This was a new development. Ricky had obtained his driver's permit and we had begun some months before his death to practice driving in the afternoons. During these sessions questions about dating and girls in general were beginning to be interspersed with questions about lane changes and the miracle of the standard shift automobile. I learned that there was someone special in his life. When we first started talking about girls I assumed that there was "a girl," someone from his school. Ricky was not willing to tell me at first that there was a special someone. For purposes of clarity and focus, I told him that this hypothetical girl needed a name. We settled on *Fontiqua*. If I refer to his girlfriend in the future, that is what she will be called. We are protecting the names of innocents and all that – understand?

Ricky became more interested in girls at the normal time for boys. About that same time he participated in a True Love Waits (15) seminar at our church. The concepts of dating, dating for the purpose of finding a life mate and being celibate until marriage rang true with him. He had seen first hand the results of promiscuous sex and more. He had seen the results of drugs and alcohol and felt no need to partake of them himself. Most of all, Ricky recognized what happens to children when their parents fail at their job. He reconfirmed a commitment to not date or go out with girls until he was ready and able to marry. He also made the commitment to finish school and get his terminal degree before he chose to marry. As he got to the age that all of the rest of his peers started noticing girls, he changed that approach a little. He wanted a relationship. He did not want to go out with a girl "just for fun" but was not opposed to having a close girl friend as long as there was not a lot of pressure for sex.

Rick's MySpace world

Ricky was seeking a separate identity from that of his adopted family. He found out that MySpace gave him a way to create a fantasy life for himself. In that way he tried to become the man he wanted to be. As you saw in earlier chapters, children who lack attachment to a parent or who have no parent will try to recreate that family unit as they grow older. It is a second chance to have an intact family. Several years in foster care and seven years in my home had never replaced that in his life. I'm convinced that he loved my wife and me and that he loved his sister. But he had reached the age when a lot of boys think, "I am almost grown. I can't wait to get out of here!" Like most adolescents, he was looking for ways to stand out among his peers. Show his stuff. Strut. Pose. The online space offered just that opportunity. He could individuate himself from his family, his friends and establish himself as a separate entity. In his case, what he learned in Computer Class at school allowed him to create a truly cool site. He was immediately accepted by his peers.

Rick learns about social networking

Ricky came to social networking in late 2004 and spent very little time on it at first. He was, at that time, still learning the computer and was very "hooked" on internet games. Like most kids we had constant discussions about whether or not he could play certain games. At that time we did not allow him to do online gaming because we had already learned about what happens when boys go into chat rooms and get recruited by freakazoids. He was only allowed to play online games with friends that visited in the home. He had a couple of pals that were regular players.

Over time he began to get interested in playing guitar. From his income working in the summer of 2004, Ricky bought an acoustic guitar. That Christmas his relatives gave him so much cash that he was able to buy an electric guitar and amplifier. We were amazed that Ricky learned the guitar so quickly. I took him to a guitar show and we bought several different guitar books so he could improve. He never took lessons but he had become so adept at the guitar that we were planning to start them right after he got his drivers license and could transport himself.

Ricky lost interest in gaming and began to use the computer to find music that fit into the guitar method he was learning. The computer can be a very good educational tool. He also began instant messaging with his buddies who played guitar. They gave each other tips and when necessary used the telephone to demonstrate what they were playing. Eventually they began to actually plan practice sessions. There was a lot of talk and planning that went into the formation of the band. Formation of the band also made him interested in the bands that were on MySpace.

Friends of Rick Rokr

A discussion of Ricky's life would be incomplete without talking about his school and extracurricular life while he was living with us. Ricky had a good group of friends in school. He was very loyal to his friends and thought of them as special. He was reluctant to introduce us to many of them – which is normal for his age. What we learned after his death is that these friends were neither the nerds nor the most popular kids from school. They were kids with character and a strong sense of right and wrong.

Between his eighth and ninth school year we moved. The new home was a couple of hundred miles away. He was apprehensive of the change but made a close group of friends pretty quickly. Ricky had that infectious smile and the ability to get along with anyone. He was pretty good about picking friends who shared his values. One of his best friends was a boy who will probably be the Valedictorian his senior year. Ricky was an active scout for almost six years. He had reached the rank of Life Scout and was planning his Eagle Scout project. Ricky had just passed his driving test and started a new job. He was already getting special assignments because he was well liked on the job. He had a keen sense of fairness and was beginning to develop character.

Ricky the Jew

Ricky had internalized the values of a new Christian and had been baptized about six years before his death. He had no problem telling others about being a Christian and got the nickname among some less spiritually focused acquaintances as "Ricky the Jew." Occasionally, he would have trouble with some aspect of religion or Christianity and discuss it with his sister. He talked to his mother and me as well. He attended church, although he would grouse about it when he wanted to do something else – which usually meant sleeping late. He reveled in his friends and many of them went to the same church as he. He tried to live a Christian life and told us often that there were conflicts between what some of his friends did and what he believed. But he was convinced that what he believed was true.

Ricky also had a large group of friends who felt like they knew him on his MySpace site. Many of them tried to speak to him through cyberspace when he posted a notice saying "today is the day I go to meet my Heavenly Father." What is important to me, as his earthly father, is that he knew that he was going to see his Heavenly Father. For those of you reading this book that are not used to Christian thought; this may be difficult for you to appreciate. Knowing Ricky, perhaps I understand the ideas that lead him to rationalize the each step and come to the conclusion that suicide would work for him – even though the ideas were flawed. Because of his early life, Ricky always had the thought in the back of his mind that someone would come to rescue him from whatever situation that he got into. They always had. Ricky was so young and was so taken care of by his older sisters that he did not feel or understand the effects of neglect in the same way in those early years. Countless adults came in and out of his parent's homes and the home of his foster parents even when the ones who were supposed to be taking care of him were not. When there are always people stepping in at the last moment, you get used to them always stepping in at the last moment. My assumption is that Ricky saw God as the ultimate rescuer who would forgive him for taking his life. The grace of God is difficult for many people to understand. But Ricky saw God as the one who would always love him, care for him and would make things right. Because of how our society always asks questions at the time of catastrophe we often think that if people follow God nothing bad will happen to them. This is certainly how it is supposed to happen with earthly parents. Do good, get good grades, and you get special privileges. But Christianity does not teach that following Christ has a cause and effect relationship with a better earthly life; 100% of the time. Yes, God will bless his followers. But the things that happen in the world are the result of the nature of the world. It is fallible. Storms, earthquakes and natural disasters happen. Evil men enslave or dominate whole populations. Christianity is a promise for comfort and peace in good and bad times and the assuredness of an eternal life. That relationship gives us comfort and helps us find strength when we are faced with some tragedy. That is a supernatural view. Ricky believed that there was a supernatural aspect to this existence. At the same time, I'm not sure that Ricky understood the finality of death. Like a lot of kids that age, Ricky knew a little bit about a lot of things and thought he was an expert on everything.

Fantasy

I have a suspicion that a conversation that we had late one evening planted the seed for what he did. Ricky and I were discussing the girl that he had been "seeing" and I mentioned that he would one day have a chance as an adult to create the family unit that he had missed out on as a child. Although his role would change, he would be a part of his own specially identified unit. It was evident that the idea appealed to him. After his death, I began to look at his MySpace site and found it true to the ideas about the future family unit we discussed that night.

I did not realize that Ricky had created a complete fantasy life for himself, crawled in and closed the door behind him. I did not understand that he could not see the difference between the fantasy he was creating and the life he was living. I had no idea that something like the myspaces existed. I did not understand that there was a processing point that would allow a child to blur the line between worlds. From my experience with children I knew that magical thinking could allow them to believe things that were illogical. In earlier chapters I discussed this in relationship to teen pregnancy and gang belief. But a place on a computer where children fell into an Alice in Wonderland world where they had real emotional responses to an unreal life? No, I did not know and was not prepared to battle anything of the sort. In this new world (according to his site) he was Rick Rokr, the lead guitarist of a rock band; he made a "couple of thousand" every other weekend playing at different clubs. The magical thinking of his peers played a role. It allowed him to convince them that he was traveling to Australia, Florida and California for "gigs." He created a promotional site for the band that he formed with his friends. It promised that they would soon be "rocking out" in a completely unique style that was a blend of Red Hot Chili Peppers and Metallica. The truth is that I heard Ricky play a lot. To be sure, he had incredibly fast fingers and could play the bridge, introduction or solos of several famous songs. His "band" had two practice sessions. *I'm not sure that he or any member of the band actually knew a single song from beginning to end.*

Rick is married on MySpace

One of the oddities of MySpace is that kids get "married on MySpace" which is roughly synonymous with 50's and 60's kids who swapped I.D. bracelets. Once the user establishes this relationship he or she changes her online biography to denote that they are now married. Congratulations come from their friends who wish them well and assure them that they will have a long life together. There is no way of determining just how much stock the users take in these relationships.

Being "married on MySpace" is one of the more bizarre things about the social networking site – to me. Perhaps that is because this is the final piece of the puzzle that led my son to take his life. I guess that is why it angers me to talk about it. However, it is a phenomenon of the social networking site that exists. It is a game that many of them play.

For Ricky this was not a game. He professed his love and Fontiqua reciprocated. They changed their profiles on their myspace sites from single to married. Reviewing all of his bulletins, I see that they received the best wishes of all their online friends. Each friend predicted that their love would last forever. On his site the word forever appears in the background wallpaper. His conversation was peppered with comments about loving her forever. He was heavily committed to this relationship.

Ricky talked to me one night about birthday presents for this girl. He told me she was about to turn sixteen and he wanted to give her something special. At the time I did not know about being married on myspace. Ricky went to a jewelry site and found a couple of rings he though were cool. He discussed it with his circle of friends and then – best I can tell – presented the ring in cyber form to Fontiqua. Later, I found out that he told his best friend that he was going to put a similar ring on layaway when he got his first check from his new job. They were married, ring and all – sort of.

It is especially heartbreaking for me that Ricky and Fontiqua were never in the same room together. They never even met in person. She lived in a town near where we had lived 2 years earlier— but they had never met. He had only seen her photograph. Ricky let himself to be caught in a magical world that allowed him to have a romance with a person he had never met. Before SNS that magical lover would not have been someone real. The imaginary lover could not carry on a conversation with you. Someone you could talk to, hang on the phone for hours with and instant message poems and words of endearment. MySpace made it possible for a perverse sort of magic to become real. Their marriage lasted for several months.

In our late night conversations he would frequently talk to me about how you make things last. A revealing look at Ricky's attitude toward life can be described in how he approached buying his electric guitar. I pointed out to him that he could get a more well-known brand of guitar if he shopped for a used one. He told me that he only wanted a guitar that no one else had ever played. He had often told me that he only wanted new things and that you could not trust used things. He did not invest in things that he did not expect to last.

What Ricky did not know was that his girlfriend had not told him the truth. She was not sixteen. She was thirteen. Her MySpace actually showed her to be 73. I suspect that was a purposeful mistake. You have to be fourteen to have a site. If you "don't know" that and "accidentally" made your one into a seven — it's just a tiny mistake that you could make your parents believe. At least you think you can when you are thirteen. A lot of girls hide their ages in this manner. From conversations I had with her mother later, I discovered that she had older sisters. In their family, fourteen was the age that they could begin dating. When this time came around the two of them began to have long conversations on the telephone. During the week before his death, I learned that the relationship was tapering off because she wanted to date other boys. Since it was just before her birthday I suspect she had changed her mind about their relationship lasting forever. She had still not told him that she was only thirteen. Had she told the truth in the first place Ricky would not have talked to her. He had always considered anyone that much younger than him a *mere child* - be they boy or girl. You may use that as an object lesson when you are having a serious talk with your teen about the importance of truth. Even small untruths can contribute to big problems.

The beginning of the end

In the months before his death, Ricky became more and more prone to take me aside as soon as I got home from work to discuss matters of importance. Sometimes it was an argument with his mother over summer reading assignments. Sometimes he wanted help with a decision. We were beginning to have a more adult relationship. Although he would not allow me into the most secret parts of his heart, he occasionally allowed a glimpse. I was praying that this would soon spill over into the relationship with his mother. She was his main support for school work and helped him maintain a list of things he needed to do. The two of them worked hard the last few weeks of school to build his faltering grades. He had picked a lot of fights with his mother over homework because of them. Those grades had faltered – I understand now, because he was being too quick to answer everyone who logged in on his myspace network of friends.

Just before his death I began to feel that he was very concerned about Fontiqua. They were breaking up. He was very concerned and I tried to explain to him that this was a natural part of breaking up. He was adamant that I was wrong. This was a special, one-of-a-kind relationship. I had no idea how right he was, since it was a relationship built on the shifting sands of small untruths. Although it was a fantasy constructed in MySpace it was built with imaginary timbers nailed to my son's heart. When the relationship began to end, he had to accept that the first investment that he had made into love was coming to an end. A promise that he had made to himself would never happen, was happening. The girl with whom he was so infatuated was moving on. Ricky was so enmeshed in this space that the alternate reality of it carried heartbreaking emotion. His reaction was that of a young married man who did not want to give up the life he had built with the girl of his dreams.

In the three days before his death, Ricky had begun a new job. He was about to get the biggest paycheck of his life. On Monday of that week he got his driver's license and was beginning to drive himself to places he had never before been to alone. He had spent a lot of time being Ricky over the last few days. On the last day of his life he spent the majority of the day on his computer talking to his friends and to his girlfriend. He had been Ricky on those three days. On that day he was Rick Rokr. Rick Rokr wrote songs, played lead guitar in a group called Audio Mayhem and made lots of money doing it. All his friends knew that. They also knew that he was married; married to the one girl who truly understood him. She had been given the opportunity to be his one-and-only. She had no idea that he meant it so fervently. When she began talking about the relationship that day, something happened. His carefully crafted world was coming apart. He was going to have to give up the one relationship that he had allowed himself to form. Yet another woman, one he had trusted completely, had failed him. His friends would know. They might also find out that he really didn't go all over the country playing guitar. School was about to start and he would have to see on a regular basis – face to face – the same people who had congratulated him for being married on MySpace. They might laugh. They might realize that the world he had created was not real and that he too, like his parents, had failed at keeping his world together. He was panicked. He made a snap decision to kill himself. After posting a melodramatic goodbye on MySpace and ignoring the pleas of his online family AND while talking to his "wife" on the phone; he took his life.

MySpace allowed him a schism in his personality that let him have a fantasy life with very real emotions and reactions to them. He had only one personality when he started using MySpace. He was a sixteen year old boy with a driver's license, a job, somewhat unlimited freedom of movement and a drop dead gorgeous smile. He had the promise of an unlimited future until he started to experiment with something that he did not realize was temporary and unstable. It makes me insane...with grief.

On the spaces, they say it takes a minute to find a special person, an hour to appreciate them and a day to love them, but an entire life to forget them. I'll never live long enough for his memory to dim.

He was a victim, a victim of biological parents consumed by drug use. He was a victim of adults (foster parents) too busy with their own needs to consider his pain. He was victim of adults too busy to properly conduct business so it was safe (MySpace). His spirit was wounded by a foster parent who was too preoccupied with her own success to meet his needs as a child. He felt abandoned by his family. He was offered a product in the form of an internet tool for making friends. He thought they were giving him the chance to make his life better. I think there is something criminal about that.

Every child that has been subjected to long term abuse, neglect or the effects of a broken home has the potential to be damaged by social networking. The potential for further wounds to their spirits, for being lead astray by bad ideas or bad people or living too long in a fantasy is high. Parents must police the use of these sites by their children. No one else will. The advertisers and providers don't want to reduce the number of users for fear that it will cut into their profits. Statistically you might think that the odds of this happening to your child are pretty low. Speaking from the point of view of being one of those statistics, it is little comfort to think that my son was in the minority. I would choose to take action rather than take a chance - if I had it to do over again. I only wish I had known what I know now.

My wife and I are professionals in the area of human and social behavior. His computer sat in a family room that was always visible to every member of the family. We thought we had protected him from pornography or the more harmful effects of internet ignorance. We had given Ricky all of the tools he needed to be successful. His time on MySpace and his relationship with this girl were making him anxious, depressed and confused and we couldn't understand why. As a result of being dehydrated, emotionally jacked up, and suffering from a lack of sleep he was briefly hospitalized. I was stunned. Why, I asked, is this reaction so intense? I had no answer because I did not know about the web site and Ricky did not have the ability to understand what was happening to him.

Ricky had never given serious thought to suicide as far as we know. None of his writings or conversation on the web sites had discussed it previously. In fact a psychiatrist interviewed him for about two hours just days before his death. The doctor found no suicidal thoughts during the wide ranging interview.

The Andrea Gail, a fishing boat, left the harbor in Gloucester, Massachusetts in 1991 and was caught in the confluence of tropical weather masses that resulted in what weather experts called the Perfect Storm. It was an event that had never happened previously. A book by that name was written about the voyage of the Andrea Gail. It gave a colloquial name to events that come together in odd or and heretofore unknown manner. Each event would have been harmless or less harmful individually. Ricky was caught is just such a perfect storm on that day in June. It happened when of a combination of minor untruths, met with a life that had suffered loss and been damaged, inside an imaginary place that had never existed before. We never knew a storm of this ferocity could take place inside a child as a result of an imaginary life, created on a website that was so new its dangers could not be assessed. I've written this book so you will have the knowledge that such an event could happen in your child's life. Only you can be the judge of how likely it would be for such an event could take place. I hope that you have learned enough to keep that ship in the harbor.

CONCLUSION

—ɯ—

So what do we do about this? I have identified what I think is the problem. It is therefore incumbent upon me to give you some sort of solution. I wish that I could tell you that I had one. Ricky died playing the role of Rick Rokr before we found a real solution. You have to know that there is a problem before you can address it.

There is no one-size-fits-all method for raising and protecting your children. That is the real answer to social networking – raise strong, critical thinkers. But, for you, I will try to give you some ideas about combating the internet. Let's start with how to control the issue of your son or daughter getting on the internet and wandering too far afield. Go to the website: www.integrity.com and do yourself a favor. Buy their annually billed internet filter service. (About $50 a year) They also offer a free tool that sends a notification to your computer when your child goes somewhere like a porn site. You can call 1.866.449.1706 and they will answer your questions. You might also try www.spectorsoft.com for minute by minute monitoring. Spectorpro 6.0 tracks where your child goes and keeps a report their website says: If you know a computer professional who knows of a better one— use it and send me a brochure.

I made the point earlier that I believe that you are nuts if you let your child have a computer in his or her bedroom. Get one of these programs and you will find out why soon enough. You can also network your computers and have a technician set up your computer so that you see exactly what your child sees at the same time. You also might want to go online and start your own social networking account and become one of your child's online friends. While you are doing it you might realize just how creepy you feel. It's easy to become a teenager again online. You can talk to teens about pretty serious stuff. Only if you get too adult or start talking weird will they deselect you as a friend. It will alarm you how easy it would be for a predator to adopt the identity of a teen and just keep shopping until he found someone willing to talk "naughty" on line.

If your children are not yet on line, teach them early that using the computer is a privilege. Don't' let them bully you because they think it is a right. Control their use and tie that to good behavior and a reward system. Never let them get the idea that it is OK to sit in front of the computer or a video game for hours. Make the computer a tool, not a toy.

A condensed version of expert advice

The various online experts say that if you are concerned about what your child might be doing on his social networking site, go look. Ask them to show you the site. If they balk, get nervous or looks like they are about to go ballistic, quickly say: "I'll give you a day or two to polish it up so it looks real nice!" You can then come back to the issue at that time. At the end of your planned session, explain that all next examination will be without warning.

This is effective, but! What my son did was become very adept at covering his tracks. I still haven't figured out what he did to the Trash Receptacle – it automatically dumps itself. He closed down his computer every night and deleted all temp files.

Keep this in mind: You should not be afraid of your kid. Just because there are electronic devices involved does not mean you lose your parent card. You're the parent. If you don't like it, unplug the computer. You have rules and they should follow them, or there should be no Internet at all. If you're not being the parent and if you're not going to step in, nothing I tell you is going to be able to help your child be safe.

You can be too "ham-fisted" about this and it will just give your child another reason to argue with you. If you choose to be a bully, they will find a way to go around you. You may have to spend some time discussing very difficult issues. After all, you are the adult, you should be able to out-think them. You should be able to take control with finesse and a caring attitude. If they suddenly want to know something scary like how one determines his sexual preference – you may have to be brave enough to say, "I don't know!" You could follow that up with a discussion of how you figured out your sexual orientation.

You should have a heart to heart talk with your child about what constitutes too much information on the SNS. Use the internet to educate yourself further. Most of the time, the fact that your child mentions he gets out of school at a certain time or that his basketball jersey number is 21 is going to sound harmless. Show him how easy it would be for a freakazoid to find him or her with that little bit of info. Teach kids to review their friends' pages and have those friends remove any personal information posted about them.

If parents discover their underage child posts to a MySpace profile, the parent can e-mail the company at "customercare@ myspace.com," and include information on the child's member name and unique Web address. MySpace will remove the profile. They will cooperate with you.

Other sources of wisdom

MySpace and SNS has a high probability of impacting how and if your child does homework. There are books that will teach you some new techniques regarding homework. I like: **Ending the Homework Hassle** , by John Rosemond. (Rosemond, 1990) This book is available at www.rosemond.com for only $10.00. When I first heard the results that parents were getting I could not believe it. It was almost too simple to be true. One of my foster parents loaned me the book. She had used it on both foster kids and her own. I have to admit is it a powerful tool. Everyone that I know has used it has improved their child's grades and their ability to deal with home-work with this one. The book teaches you to turn the responsibility for grades and study over to the kiddo. It also tells you to use things like the computer to give him or her incentive. That is, no grades, no computer. Keeping them grounded in the real world is a good way to teach balance and not make a mistake with social networking sites.

Take a page or two from the behavioral management textbooks. Spend as much time to build a relationship with your child as possible. If you are one of those who thinks that it's "your way or the highway" be prepared for the sound of a slamming door. Kids will do just about anything for someone they respect. You can't get their respect by shouting at them. Do chores *with* them. Don't have them do chores *for* you – or as you may choose to convince yourself – *for their own good*. When you want them to do something – ask. Ordering them to do things is counterproductive. If this sounds like something that is more politically correct than effective parenting, think of it this way. These are tactics. Just like in police work we have the Special Weapons and Tactics team, you have procedures that make things work. Think of adolescence is a time of crisis and use slightly different tactics. The goal, regardless how different the tactic, is to you're your child on track. Also, at about 13 you should be starting to prepare your child to make his way into the world. The absolute authority you enjoyed when he or she was a toddler is melting away. That is a good thing. They should be able to think for themselves. If you have to use a different approach during adolescence so be it. Remember what you think is right and wrong is actually the will of God. It is He who gave us the rules and He allows freedom of choice. If you travel a lot or don't get home early enough to spend much time with them – change jobs. I know you think it is just not economically feasible but you can make it happen. Your child will become a new person if you do. He or she may never become the person you hoped if you do not.

Parents should understand that your experience and knowledge are not always appreciated by your children. Every time they talk to you they are not looking to get answers. They may just want you to listen. They do not need you to analyze everything they do and give advice. They sometimes just want you to listen, so: ***just listen.***

Sneak Attack

When you walk by your child seize him or her and hug the stuffing out of them without saying any more than I love you. Of course I don't mean to do this every time you walk by them. But get in the habit of doing it regularly enough that they look forward to it. Don't' do it in front of anyone else – especially not a school buddy and especially if you have a boy. Men should hug the stuffing out of both their girls and their boys, even if they are mature, worldly and standoffish older teens. If they want you to say more, they will ask. Make night time hugs, daily mealtime prayer and holding hands a daily occurrence. As they grow older, show them some appreciation for who they are becoming. You may have to accept that the star linebacker you wanted to raise has become a pretty good thespian with a knack for languages. Your dream of having a star football player is *your* dream. If you can't accept that they are becoming what they want to be, they will interpret that as criticism and judgment. Keep your dreams to yourself.

Never be critical of their friends even if you are right. About half the time they know the kid is inappropriate. Half of that time they are hanging out with them just to see your reaction. On the other hand your kid may be trying to influence the kid you think has a bad reputation. Being critical of their friends is the same thing as being critical of your child. Most of the time they choose friends that they think fit them. Their friends are not random accidental alliances. The loyalty to their friends not only makes **their friends important**, it makes them **more important than you** during adolescence. Don't force your child to choose between you. Be confident that they actually respect the rules you have taught them over the years. Once they get through adolescence they will return to you. You will not be the first parent to notice: "My kids thought I got smarter after they got out of high school." It is funny because it is universally true.

Recognize that adolescent life is tough

Adolescence is a rough period in a child's life. James Dobson makes the comment that the 14 to 15 year bracket is a period that is so difficult that you may not feel you make any progress with your child during that time. He suggests that you have succeeded if you just get them through it alive. I have to tell you that the truth of that statement hits me particularly hard. My son never fully understood that we were not trying to keep him from accomplishing the things he really wanted; that he was not being tied down. We were just trying to create a really well built launching pad so that at the end of the countdown he could rocket to the stars.

Kids worry about some of the same things you do during the day. You would like to go to lunch with your boss. It is a sign that you are on the right track in your career if he feels comfortable around you. Your kid really does not want to eat alone and worries that no one will sit with him. I was amazed at how many of Ricky's friends identified themselves by saying: "I sat with him at his lunch table." Or "We always ate lunch together." They worry. You have to acknowledge that the things they worry about, although they may sound trivial, are important. Don't make the mistake of discounting the rites of passage at this age. Many children will remember disappointments and mean or embarrassing things said to them by parents and peers, in their old age, with the same emotional impact as the birth of their first child.

Praise

Find ways to praise them even if you have to thank them for shutting the door properly. Teach them that rules are important and that following them has a reward. You cannot punish a child into greatness. When we train foster parents in my agency we teach a reward system. When the foster parents get a difficult child in their home, they naturally tend to use the four techniques we teach for discipline: redirection and counseling, loss of privileges, time outs and early bedtimes. After a while parenting becomes timeout, timeout, timeout and timeout. Then they complain that the system will not let them spank the children. As a case manager, I have to go back and explain that the discipline system we teach is based on reward and not punishment. We teach "no's" by rewarding "yes." *You cannot have television time, until you finish your homework. If you do that quickly and without arguing, I'll make you an ice cream sundae. If you finish your homework every day this week before dinner, on Friday we will have Pizza Night. You get to choose the pizza toppings even if it's pineapple and bacon. If you earn four pizza nights in a row, you get to have pizza night at Chuckee Cheese's.* With pre-adolescents, parents get all wound up in the idea that this is bribery. My reaction is: "You say that like it is a bad thing?" A little grease – even if it is pizza grease – makes things run more smoothly. It's a *tactic*, remember! You can always resort to force or punishment much later in the discussion.

What you are teaching is that obedience has a positive outcome. You are saying: Do my will and you will be rewarded. You are not saying: Do this thing and you will get a pizza. There is a subtle but important difference. This is, quite frankly, what God tries to tell us. Do God's will and there will be a positive outcome. Read Psalms and Proverbs; those two books are full of promises of reward for obedience. In Proverbs you will find that rebellion is as natural for a child as breathing. You are an adult, you are supposed to understand that rebellion is expected – and to me at least – welcome. I like to fish and when the fish has the line pulled tight, I know the chances of my landing him are pretty good. I've got to keep the line tight, take my time real fast, and work it toward my goal – getting it in the boat. Most of the time, I just put him back to fight another day. Your child has to face the world and a thousand temptations. You have got to keep the line of communication tight even though your quarry is fighting hard. Even if that communication does not always seem to work; when your quarry pulls more line out than you expected; if you keep the line tight but not too tight, you keep connected. The hook or connection is lost when the line goes limp. You are an adult; you are supposed to have learned some finesse. Bribery is finesse, punishment is a sledgehammer. One of the most valuable lesions I ever learned was from a City Manager who commented: "We call you (the police) only when every other method of dealing with a problem (negotiation) has been exhausted. When your people come in (force) every other option has been tried."

Attend Church Regularly

Take your child to church. We started just going to services and Sunday Morning Bible Study. But the kids were quickly invited to other events. Once my children began going to church events, I found that I enjoyed going with them. Then we learned to like to go to in-depth Bible study together and talk about the Bible in the home. We learned to base our lives on those principles. What they learned, I learned. As a result we had a lot of time driving to and from events talking about what we learned. We had a relationship with each other and with Christ.

When my daughter, Ricky's sister, accepted Christ she had one of the most profound conversion experiences I have ever witnessed. She went from being a somewhat emotionally disturbed teen that would have a major tantrum every 45 days, to being a new creature. She began a relationship with Christ and began a new life of her own. She is now a junior in College, studying to be an engineer so she can build churches and roads in rural Mexico. She hopes to use those talents to be a missionary to the Indian tribes. You have to love a kid like that!

Having that relationship will allow you to mold and direct your child in a way that no Dr. Spock or home spun advice about washing their mouths with soap can. Learn to let God orchestrate our life. You will be glad you did.

REFERENCES

—ᴍ—

Boeree, C. George (1997) <u>Personality Theories</u> ww.ship. edu/~cgboeree/erikson 2006

Crain, William <u>Theories of Development</u> Prentice Hall, Englewood Cliffs, New Jersey 1992 3rd Edition

Delaterre, Edwin J. Character and Cops, Ethics in Policing, American Enterprise Institute for Public Policy Research, Washington, D.C. 1994

Dobson, James (2001) <u>Bringing up Boys</u> Tyndale House Publishers, Wheaton, Illinois <u>www.tyndale.com</u>

Federman, Mark, Robert Nanders Blogging on *Apophenia: spatial nature of MySpace* June 2, 2006 <u>http://www.zephoria.org/ thought/archives/2006/06/02/spatial_nature.html</u>

Freud, S (1923)<u>The Ego and the id</u>, (J.Roviere, trans.). New York: W.W. Norton & Co. 1960

Guttmacher, Alan, Alan Guttmacher Institute (AGI) 1999 Facts in Brief. Teen sex and pregnancy [online] <u>www.agi-usa.org/ pubs/fb teen sex.html</u>

Jung, C.G. (1945) <u>The relations between the ego and the uncon-scious</u> (R.F.C Hull trans.) In the Collected Works of C.G.

Jung (Volume VII) *Two Essays in Analytic Psychology* Princeton: Princeton University Press (1953)

Larsen, J (1980) <u>Bundy: The Deliberate Stranger</u> Pocket; Rep/Mv Tie edition, Simon & Schuster, New York

Morgan, Erin <u>Adolescents and Sex</u> Research Associate, Assistant Professor and Huyebner, Angela, Human Development, Virginia Tech Publication Number 350-853, Posted November 2002

Mullis, Ronald L (2003) <u>Relations between Identity Formation and Family Characteristics among Young Adults</u> Journal of Family Issues, Vol. 24, No. 8, SAGE Publications

Rosemond, John, (1990) <u>Ending the Homework Hassle</u> Andrews and McNeel a Universal Press Synidicate Company, 4530 Main Street, Kansas City, Missouri 64111

Silberman, C., (1978) <u>Criminal Violence, criminal justice</u> Bantam Press, New York

Slattery, John reporting in New York , WCBS News Online, Sep 18, 2006 7:53 pm US/Eastern <u>http://wcbstv.com/</u>

Troyka, Lynn Quitman *Simon and Schuster Handbook For Writers* 1999 Prentice-Hall, Upper Saddle River, New Jersey 07458

Wallerstein, R.S. and Goldberger, Leo (1998) <u>Ideas and Identities: The Life and Work of Erik Erikson</u> International Universities Press Madison, CT

Waters, T.J. Class 11: <u>Inside the CIA's First Post-9/11 Spy Class</u> Dutton, 2006 ISBN: 0525949291

Watson, Joshua C. <u>Internet Addiction Diagnosis and Assessment: Implications for Counselors</u> (pg. 17) Journal of Professional

Counseling: Practice, Theory & Research, Volume 33, Number 2 Fall 2005 Published by the Texas Counseling Association, 1204 San Antonio, St. 201 Austin, Texas 78701 www.txca.org

Witmer, Denise The National Institute on Drug Abuse (NIDA). ©2006 About, Inc., A part of The New York Times Company. All rights reserved.

ENDNOTES

—ᴡᴡ—

(1) See: Andrews, Michelle, Decoding MySpace, U.S. News and World Report, Page 46-60, September 18, 2006

(2) Dann-Courtney, Priscilla My Daughter's "space." Denver Post. Launched 6/22/2006 – DenverPost.com

(3) Hollywood Reporter, July 25, 2006, *MySpace a launch pad for next-gen media biz* News Corp. charts 'what's next By Diane Mermigas www.hollywoodreporter.com

(4) Slattery, John reporting in New York , WCBS News Online, Sep 18, 2006 7:53 pm US/Eastern http://wcbstv.com/

(5) Denise Witmer, *Source:* The National Institute on Drug Abuse (NIDA).©2006 About, Inc., A part of The New York Times Company. All rights reserved.

(6) www.coolnurse.com/alcohol.htm

(7) The National Suicide Prevention Lifeline is a 24-hour, toll-free suicide prevention service available to anyone in suicidal crisis. If you need help, please dial 1-800-273-TALK (8255). You will be routed to the closest possible crisis center in your area. With over 120 crisis centers across the country, our mission is to provide immediate assistance to anyone seeking mental health services. Call for yourself, or someone you care about. Your call is free and confidential.

Why should I call the Lifeline?

From immediate suicidal crisis to information about mental health, crisis centers in our network are equiped to take a wide range of calls. Some of the reasons to call 1-800-273-TALK are listed below.

- Call to speak with someone who cares
- Call if you feel you might be in danger of hurting yourself
- Call to find referrals to mental health services in your area
- Call to speak to a crisis worker about someone you're concerned about.

(34) It would be hard to find one single source or one single place to put it for the work done by Erik Erikson (1902 – 1994) that is paraphrased in this chapter of the book. Suffice to say that most of these principles were first assembled by him from Freud's work. If you have that inclination, I suggest reading any or all of his work. See also (Wallerstein, R.S. and Goldberger, Leo (1998) Ideas and Identities: The Life and Work of Erik Erikson International Universities Press Madison, CT

(9) Troyka, Lynn Quitman *Simon and Schuster Handbook For Writers* 1999 Prentice-Hall, Upper Saddle River, New Jersey 07458

(10) Alan Guttmacher Institute (AGI) 1999 Facts in Brief. Teen sex and pregnancy [online] www.agi-usa.org/pubs/fb teen sex.html

(11) ABC News, Feb 1, 2005

(12) Finder, Alan For Some, Online Persona Undermines a Résumé, June 11, 2006, New York Times Online

(13) Game Description: This game delves into the morning of April 20th, 1999 and asks players to relive that day through the eyes of Eric Harris and Dylan Klebold, those responsible for the deadliest school shooting in American history.

Artist's Statement : When I discovered a program called RPG Maker, I knew I had to achieve my childhood ambition of designing a video game. The question of what the game's subject would be came almost instantly; a striking event from my own formative years tugged at my instincts to make the "unthinkable" game. . . . As humanity teeters precariously on the threshold of collapse—politically, ideologically, and environmentally, the days of comatose media coverage and a subservient populace cannot remain. Eric Harris and Dylan Klebold, through their furious words and malevolent actions, can be understood as **the canaries in the mine**—foretelling of an **"apocalypse soon"** for those remaining to ponder their deeds. With 'Super Columbine Massacre RPG!,' I present to you one of the darkest days in modern history and ask, "**Are we willing to look in the mirror?**" *Danny Ledonne, from the Super Columbine RPG site.*

(43) *Joint Statement on the Impact of Entertainment Violence on Children, Congressional Public Health Summit, July 26, 2000 American Pediatric Association*

(14) Fourteen Texas Legislators fled the state in 2003 and tried to hide out in a hotel in Oklahoma. The purpose being that it was out of jurisdiction of those who would have been able to subpoena them back to session. Their absence kept the Texas House from enacting legislation for weeks.

(15) True Love Waits® is one of several approaches to challenging teenagers and college students to make a commitment to sexual abstinence until marriage. Created by LifeWay Christian Resources, True Love Waits is designed to encourage moral purity by adhering to biblical principles. This youth-based international campaign utilizes positive peer pressure by encouraging those who make a commitment to refrain from pre-marital sex to challenge their peers to do the same. http://www.lifeway.com/tlw/

APPENDIX

—◦◦◦—

Sandwiched in with all of the teens looking for approval for their new hair cut or the outfit they plan to wear the first day of the next school year are weirder places. How weird do you want to get? Try these:

Mydeathspace.com

This little personal space was put up by a twenty-something young man working in the legal profession. It aims to eulogize users of social networking spaces that have died. Supposedly, this is a serious attempt to make a place for people to be remembered. Since any person who comments on the dearly departed is protected by the anonymity of the social space moniker, some pretty crude and insensitive remarks are posted as well.

In the defense of the young man who created the space, he did call police when a young person called him to "request a reservation" for herself because she was suicidal. From my own reading, about the least likely place that a person should look to for support and encouragement is a social networking site.

Nature Witch

This site is just a friendly neighborhood introduction to witchcraft. Don't be alarmed it's only "green" witchcraft. This is just a sample of what your child can learn:

People literally leap the fire, leaving behind negative behaviors or influences. In farming communities, animals were often herded between two fires to ensure their fertility in the coming mating season. Couples may be handfasted on this day, choosing to celebrate the God and Goddess aspect within themselves on this holy day of union. Appropriate rituals for this holiday include those outlined above, as well as rituals celebrating love between yourself and your partner. You may also want to do work in the physical world to help nature grow, such as tree planting, working in a garden, or other ecological volunteer work. Beltane, or Beltaine, is the celebration of two powers joining to bring creation, in this case, the Goddess and the God. The two form a sacred union, from which comes creation, growth and harmony.

Dumb Pervert Criminal

This is not really a site, but it is a story worth telling. There is a recurring story on the web that can be traced to an incident in Jacksonville, Florida in which an adult male contacted what he thought was an eighteen year old girl. They met at a local apartment complex. He gave her a description of what he would be driving. When he arrived, two fourteen year old girls robbed him at gunpoint. There is some ironic justice in that one.

Flirtomatic

In the United Kingdom the site, Flirtomatic is a social networking spin-off that is dedicated to flirting. There was no mention if there were any age requirements, confirmation of marital status or any other safeguards. But they do hope to spread the word "virally." They mean by "word of mouth" and through other users.

Vampire Freaks.com

Besides the fact that this is the site that Kimveer Gill used, it is an oddly un-weird site. The fellow that started it is a computer whiz and Goth junky who likes Industrial Bands. I like Japanese drums and there is something similar and likeable in the clanging and rhythmic noise of these bands. He likes Vampires too, but I didn't see any advertising for Type O negative or tooth sharpening. It is an alternate identity site that contains multiple opportunities for the members to purchase Goth related material. This is not a site that a lot of Christians will be signing on – but it is a lot more like all the rest than you would first guess. It's about making money off of one of the many weird things that people choose to do – rather than accept the fact that God has a plan for your life. WDE

Wildthing:

Wildthing is just one of the sites that cover this sort of material. It is a long way from the SNS idea of making friends. Read on if you are courageous.

Wild Thing's Blurbs: "IF YOU ARE 14-15 YOU MUST FRIEND ME BEFORE EMAILING ME......JUST GIRLS LOOKING TO HAVE FUN AND GET WET -n- WILD" NO GUYS WILL BE ADDED DO YOU SEE ANY GUYS ON MY FRIEND LIST GET A CLUE

Others that wont be added
1. people with no pics
2. people with only one pic - this are fakes
3. people that are not here to have fun all other are added and will have a hot time

I have been a lesbian all my life... never liked boys, even in jr high. I started off with a friend down the street when I was very, very young…and never stopped. I like to be the one doing the licking... and watching my partner have fun. I can go all night long...and most nights I do. I get to sleep about 6am each morning after a long fun night.

I have never met a girl that can go as long as I can...they always need to stop for a break after hours of play time. I am just horny all the time....and like to make others VERY happy. I love to give straight girls a couple of drinks and turn them lez…it is easy to do. You get them hot and they will let you do anything to them...

This is my second time to be a senior...so I get to control all the freshman girls.. I love to teach the younger ones how to have fun at parties...

I live with my 16yr gf and her 31yr mother.... my girl will do anything I ask to anyone I want..... It has made for some fun parties at the house.... Everyone knows what can go on and they play along … right in front of everyone.

Funny A—ed Bitch

About me:

I'm a crazy crazy girl and I finally made a myspace cuz I like meeting new people and I'm always getting fun and funny stuff online and I thought I'd share it someplace.

Click below for the full news report & please re-post this story to help spread the word of caution that YES, even people on tv will try to get you drunk and have sex with you (and in this case video tape it) even if you are 13............

The FAB above tells you this story by way of introduction. She is trying to say that the porn site you are about to witness is a result of her being drunk and photographed without her knowledge or consent. You will notice that she is also saying that she was only 13 at the time. While this is probably not true— if it were, anyone possessing this material would be subject to prosecution for a felony. An icon on this site took me directly to a choice of porn sites. It was up front about the fact that I was going to need a credit card at least. WDE

Little Lola

Hi I am Lola, am 18 and from Europe. This is my fan club website. In here you will see me and my adventures with older men and my bi-sexual girlfriends. I have always been a very sexual person, and meeting HornyBill has allowed me to express my wildest fantasies. Members of the site will get to see the kinky games we play, such as my surprise gyno exam by a clown, my love of costume play (and was a gorilla involved!) and my many randy adventures with my friends. You will also see lots and lots of my video clips and image sets that are available no where else, and will give you a sneak peek at my diary so you will know some of the dirty things I am up to. I look forward to seeing you inside.

I am now looking for girls to have fun with, even if just to talk. But I also am hoping to find some cuties out there that if they are 18 or older who might wanna work with me. I am looking for girls like me and Teena, the Marsha Brady types who look sweet and wholesome. I want to do some erotic photography and am hoping to find models. I also am going to do the website design. It seems to me a girl should be more comfortable working with another girl and could make some good money working with me and we have a blast doing it! So please if you are thinking about doing any erotic modeling - email me - and lets talk! Also need to add here am not interested in working with guys SORRY!

Naked Nancy

I'm Naked Nancy, And I'm on my WebCam! Wanna see? Then come play with me

it's free, it's fun and its only for adults :) (18) I'll be on for awhile Come watch!

Im 21 years old and live in Chicago, Ill. I spend alot of time on my webcam and I love for people to watch me.

COLOPHON

—⸙—

The author of this book is Woody Edmiston, a career law enforcement professional. He has been a police executive in two communities, holds Master's status with the Texas Commission on Law Enforcement Officer Standards and Education and a Master's Degree from Southwest Texas State University. He has an undergraduate degree from Dallas Baptist University in Social Work and Business marketing. He has been active in the Boy Scouts of America and served on Youth Committee's in several churches.

Following the adoption of his two children he became an advocate of "older child" adoption for persons who have already raised children. Mr. Edmiston is now employed full-time in adoption services. He teaches certification courses for foster parents.

The messages in the book are drawn from personal experiences and where possible, references have been made to statistical or scientific work that supports the anecdotal evidence.

If this booklet finds popular circulation, that will be in the hands of the Creator.

www.ingramcontent.com/pod-product-compliance
Lightning Source LLC
Chambersburg PA
CBHW051054050326
40690CB00006B/711

* 9 7 8 1 6 0 0 3 4 9 9 2 8 *